£1.35

Calling All Guides

Photo: Surrey Advertiser

SBN 361 035136
Copyright © 1976 by PURNELL BOOKS,
Berkshire House, Queen Street, Maidenhead, Berks.
Made and printed in Great Britain by Purnell & Sons Ltd.,
Paulton and London

*Cover photo shows Alison Smith of the 1st Prestwood Company, Bucks.
Front endpaper photographs by Janet Harber and* Kentish Times; *back endpaper photographs by Mrs Houghton and* Dudley Herald

THE
GIRL GUIDE
ANNUAL 1977

Published by special arrangement with
THE GIRL GUIDES ASSOCIATION

PURNELL

Girls would be Boys if they could

**Do You Agree?
Asks the Editor**

In the United States of America girls are trying to break into the Boy Scout movement. Yes, although there is a flourishing Girl Scout organisation, millions strong, girls are trying to overcome the official Boy Scout policy of "boys only" and become Boy Scouts.

The Boy Scouts of America flatly refuse to admit girls, pointing out that the Girl Scouts are for girls and the Boy Scouts for boys. This seems reasonable and logical, but it doesn't satisfy the militant misses of Massachusetts and Missouri. One older girl, who is a member of an Explorer Unit in Connecticut, earned twenty-one merit badges, which would entitle a boy to become an Eagle Scout, but this accomplished young lady's application for an Eagle badge was turned down because she was not a member of the Boy Scout movement, only a participant in what in Britain we call "joint activities".

You can guess how strongly some of these girls-would-be-boys advocates feel on the subject when you learn that there is even talk of legal action against the Boy Scouts of America on the ground of sex discrimination! I ask you!

Many boy-type activities, as the director of the Boy Scouts of America points out, are not suited to girls, nor attractive to them, and of course many pursuits and pastimes beloved by girls would be unacceptable to boys. It seems to me that the masculine and feminine mentality and outlook differ so much that it would not be possible to contrive a programme of activities that would fit the needs of boys and girls at the same time.

Another point to consider and one that the feminine would-be Scouts haven't apparently noticed is—would the boys, the Scouts themselves, accept girls in their numbers? In America girls are allowed to take part in some Cub Scout activities, despite there being a flourishing Brownie Scout organisation, but they are not permitted to become Cub Scouts. If they were admitted as Scouts, it could mean a draining-away of boys from the Boy Scout Movement!

In Great Britain and America women are warranted as Cub Scout Leaders, but when it has been suggested that there should be women Leaders for Scouts the idea has not so far been well received, though I personally know of one Scout Troop, in my own county, that was saved from disbandment when its Leader left and a lady stepped into the breach and ran the Troop with outstanding success.

Still, Leaders are rather different from girls as Scouts in the Troop. Would all the boys leave, or would they like it, or would they just grin and bear it? What do *you* think?

In Great Britain the Guides and the Scouts carry on very separate and distinct programmes, though basic activities like camping are

common to both. I have never heard of girls agitating to be Scouts since the pioneer days of the Crystal Palace rally, when girls pressed their determination to share in the great Movement B.-P. founded for boys by turning up uninvited and so alerted B.-P. to the need for a similar organisation for girls, to which, of course, he responded by asking his sister, Agnes, to organise one.

But perhaps my ear isn't close enough to the ground and I haven't heard a growing rumble inside and outside the Guide hall indicative of a widespread longing on the part of girls to be boys and, especially, Scouts.

Mind you, I don't believe it! My own experience tells me that the three hundred thousand or so Guides in Great Britain are well satisfied with their Movement, thoroughly enjoy being Guides, have no wish to be Scouts, and are content to confine masculine-type pursuits to those within the range of "joint activities" with Scouts.

But you are the Guides—what do *you* think?　　　**—R.M.**

Guides and Scouts pitch a tent blindfold at a joint Guide-Scout camp near Bedford

Photo: Bedford County Press

THE PERM

by A. I. Duncan

"That's the lot," came Jill's voice from under the platform.

It was Wednesday evening, and as usual the 2nd Braniel Girl Guide Company was meeting in the church hall. The following weekend was Lyn's Patrol Camp Permit test, and the Daffodil Patrol was borrowing from the Company's camp equipment stored under the platform.

"Gosh!" gasped Ann, surveying the crowded floor. "You'd think the whole Company was going for a week's camp!"

"Oh, do give over, Ann!" her twin, Joan, replied. "We're not taking all this equipment; we have to sort it out yet."

"Well, for Pete's sake let's get on with it or we'll be here all night," said Isla, pushing her way between the twins. "Where's your list, Lyn?"

Lyn, the Patrol Leader, who was struggling with a pile of dixies and looking for somewhere on the already crowded floor to dump them, answered between puffs, "Over there, Isla, under the poles for number-three tent."

Just then the slightly bored voice of the Patrol Second, Enid, was heard to say, "Well, really! Shall we ever be ready? Just look at all this mess!"

"Of course we'll be ready," said Isla, "but if we had to depend on your help it might be next year before we are!"

Enid had the grace to colour; she always felt at a loss with Isla, never seeming to come out on top in any argument. The rest of the Guides looked at one another, knowing that Enid was still angry at not being chosen Patrol Leader of the Daffodil Patrol. She had been "playing up" to Skipper (the name chosen by the Company for their Guider), hoping she would have influenced the Patrol to vote for her, and was annoyed when Skipper left the decision to the members of the Patrol themselves. What really puzzled the Patrol was why Enid had been chosen by Lyn as her Second when Isla was her best friend and very popular with the other Guides. Lyn would certainly have preferred Isla, but

Skipper had talked to her and said she thought the responsibility of being a Patrol Second would help Enid to become a better Guide. Skipper thought half the trouble with Enid was "parent trouble", or at least "mother trouble". Her mother was so busy with coffee mornings, charity work, committee meetings and so on that she had little time for Enid and tried to make up for her lack of attention by showering her daughter with material things. Most of the other girls in the Patrol had no time for Enid and her high-handed manner. Jill was the exception. Jill was the youngest member of the Patrol and greatly impressed by Enid. She hung on every word Enid uttered, and constantly sought her company. Jill wasn't strong and couldn't join in the boisterous type of game the Daffodil Patrol seemed to prefer. Enid didn't often join in these games, either, but for a different reason—unless she was chosen the "leader" or "captain"

WEEKEND

of the game she didn't wish to play. This meant that Jill and Enid were very often in each other's company.

The Patrol Permit test was being held at Knockagh, the Guides Association's camp-site about six miles from Braniel. The Guides were to be taken down to the site by one group of parents and brought back home by another. Enid, however, decided she would make her own arrangements about getting down and would bring Jill with her. She could not, of course, consider carrying any of the equipment!

The sleeping-tent and store-tent were already pitched when Enid and Jill arrived, and Lyn had to stop herself from saying "Hear, hear!" when Ann welcomed them by saying "Better late than never, I suppose", and Joan added with sarcasm, "Do you really think so?"

"Now that you *have* arrived, you could start digging the fireplace," Lyn said. "You, Jill, go with Joan and Ann for wood and bricks."

"Oh, yes, I would get the hard job, wouldn't I?" Enid moaned.

"If you had been here on time you could have chosen your job, but you weren't, so get digging," snapped Isla.

Lyn bit her lip and turned away. She knew things would not run smoothly this weekend, but she was determined to get her Permit so that the Patrol could camp together.

After Colours and prayers next morning, Lyn gave each member of the Patrol her duties for that day. Enid was given the task of deciding which gadgets should be made and where they would be used. Lyn wisely gave this job to Enid, knowing she was very capable and efficient at gadget-making. When she wanted, Enid could be an excellent Guide.

Jill and Ann helped her, and before long the sleeping-tent had its bed-rack, shoe-rack and a couple of handy little table-tops made from old garden bamboo canes snake-lashed to rest on four forked sticks. In fact, everything was off the ground as it should be in a very short time. Even the store-tent had all the stores raised off the ground on gadgets and the kitchen area boasted a fine washing-up table.

Lyn and Enid had arranged a wide game for the Patrol in the form of a treasure hunt, with the clues going via the beach to the nearest village and returning to camp by the road. At the beach they intended having their sandwiches and a paddle. When Lyn went to the tester to give the details of her intended programme, the tester advised against going by the beach because very high tides had been forecast and the beach path could be completely submerged; to use it that day could be quite dangerous, as they could be cut off. When Lyn went back to her Patrol to tell them of the change of plans, Enid was furious and blamed Lyn for not really wanting to go by the beach because she, Enid, had planned that route and worked out all the clues.

When the time came for them to set off, Enid complained

9

of feeling unwell. She said Jill had volunteered to stay and look after her.

Lyn had no option but to leave the two behind.

The Patrol had only gone about ten minutes when Enid left the tent and joined Jill outside.

"Oh, Enid, do you think you should get up yet?" Jill asked, with concern. "I thought you had gone to sleep. A good sleep would help you get well."

"Shut up, Jill, for goodness sake! I'm not ill. I only faked."

"Faked?" gasped Jill. "But why, Enid?"

"I wasn't going by the road when I had gone to the bother of preparing clues for the beach route. It was only because I had made the arrangements that Lyn decided not to go that way."

"Oh, no, Enid, that isn't true!"

"Give over, Jill!" Enid interrupted. "I'm going to go by the beach, and when we meet up with the Patrol at Cultra it will prove that I was right and Lyn was only being mean."

"We?" Jill asked, rising from her groundsheet. "You mean I am to go with you?"

"But of course! Didn't you promise your P.L. you would look after me? As a good Guide, you

"Shut up, Jill! I'm not ill. I only faked"

Enid tried to hurry Jill without alarming her

can't let me go off on my own, can you?"

"I suppose you're right, Enid, but I don't like it," replied a worried Jill. "Shall we leave a message?"

"We don't have time for that," snapped Enid. "Do make a move or they will be back before we even get started."

Enid went into the tent to get her rucksack. Jill had been making gadgets from sticks. These she now formed into an arrow and pointed them towards the beach.

Enid and a reluctant Jill made their way down the lane leading to the beach. The day had become quite windy and overcast, with grey clouds scurrying across the sky. The waves out in the bay were all white-tipped. Even Enid was taken aback at the size of the waves and the force of the wind as they turned from the sheltered

path on to the open beach, but she forced herself to answer casually when Jill timidly said, "Can't we turn back? It is much too chilly and windy to go by the beach today."

"Don't be silly, Jill! A little breeze won't do us any harm. Besides, we'll be sheltered by the high Demesne wall."

When they turned on to the beach there was no path as such; the way round the bay was over the sand. On their right was the sea, which usually rolled gently half way up the sandy beach. Today it was dashing towards the wall on their left. The sea seldom reached the wall; so usually it was safe to walk this way towards the village. Today, however, the sea was rapidly enveloping the beach like a hand with long, white-foamed fingers.

If they hurried, Enid hoped they

would cross the small stream that divided this bay from the next, when they would be able to climb the roughly made steps that led from the beach to a path high enough to be safe from the sea.

Enid tried, unsuccessfully, to hurry Jill without alarming her. It was a very unpleasant day now, the sky grey and menacing, the wind chilling. Jill was beginning to show signs of strain.

"I do wish we had never come this way; in fact, I wish we had never left the camp-site," Jill said. "Lyn was right about the tide; I've never known the sea come so far up before. Look behind us! We can't get back now. If we aren't careful, we'll be pinned against the wall."

"Shut you, can't you! If you had got a move on instead of groaning and dragging me back we would have been round this bay ages ago," snapped Enid. She herself felt alarmed now. She knew they could be cut off. They must hurry!

"I'm afraid!" Jill cried. "I want to go back to camp."

"Well, you can't, can you? The way back is cut off."

Jill, now really upset, burst into tears.

"Please, Jill, don't cry. It will only make you feel worse. I didn't mean to be nasty. We'll be okay. Just around this curve, across the stream and into the next bay, we'll be up the steps to the path. We'll stop there to rest and have some sandwiches. We can even put up our emergency shelter."

Enid hoped she spoke with more conviction than she really felt. She was now almost afraid to turn the curve in case the stream was uncrossable. She knew now this could quite easily be the case. She had never seen the sea come so high up the beach before.

When they turned the curve of the bay her worst fears were realised. The usually narrow and shallow stream that trickled down under the stone bridge between the bays from the woods above was now a fast-flowing, turbulent river about six feet across and getting bigger by the minute. They both stared at it in horror.

If only they could cross the river, and the other bay had not yet been flooded by the sea, they could get to the high path; but Enid knew that even if she could manage it Jill would never dare to cross it.

Jill knew things were wrong now. She clung to Enid, her breath coming in gasps. Enid was wise enough to realise that she and she alone was responsible for the predicament they were now in and that she and she alone would have to find a way out.

If they could not get across to the other bay and safety then she must do something here. She looked around and saw some rocks close to the high wall and beside the bridge. She coaxed Jill along to them and pushed her up on to them. The rocks were not as high as she would have liked, but at

She pushed Jill up on to the rocks

least they were higher than the rest of the beach—now being quickly submerged by the angry sea. Even the river had joined the sea, and the only dry land in the bay was their rocks. Rain was falling now, and it was being blown into them by driving wind. Very soon both girls were wet through. They had nothing with them but sweaters. Enid had intended being away only long enough to prove to Lyn that it was quite safe to go by the beach. Enid knew now that

Lyn had really been thinking of Jill, knowing she couldn't always keep up with the others. In desperation, she encouraged Jill to climb to the top of the rocks, where she put her groundsheet over them. By this time the water was already reaching their feet.

The change in the weather had made Lyn and the Patrol return to camp earlier than planned. There they found Enid and Jill were missing. Where could they be? Their anoraks were still in the tent, so they couldn't have gone far. They must have taken shelter somewhere and would be back soon. Then Ann found Jill's tracking-sign pointing towards the beach. Lyn immediately guessed what had happened and ran to the tester, Miss Murphy. Quickly and efficiently Miss Murphy organised things. Leaving some P.L.'s at the camp-site to have blankets and hot soup ready, she collected ropes and the first-aid kit and took Lyn and her Patrol with her towards the beach. She sent another group to report to the police.

As they made their way towards the beach the girls were quiet, hoping the bay would not be cut off. When they reached the end of the lane, their fears were realised. They could not get round the bay, as the sea had already reached the wall and was pounding against it. It would have been impossible for anyone to swim round the bay without being dashed against the wall.

Miss Murphy remembered the stream that ran through the estate down towards the beach and divided the two bays. If they could follow the stream under the bridge they would be able to see both bays. So they hurried back up the lane over the gate into the Demesne and headed towards the stream. Miss Murphy sent two Guides on to tell the Squire.

They knew when they reached the stream, now like a rushing river, that the sea must have almost completely engulfed the bays. The only way to see the bays was to wade or swim down the river under the bridge. This was

Quickly and efficiently, Miss Murphy organised things

13

Lyn saw two figures huddled together, with the sea surging round them

much too dangerous with the river in the raging state it was in; a swimmer could be swept right out into the bay and out to sea.

"Miss Murphy, if you would tie the rope round me and hold it on the bank I could make my way down the river and see if there is any sign of Enid and Jill," said Lyn.

"Much as I dislike the risks, it looks like the only way. I would go, but my weight might be too much for you to hold."

Lyn shook off her boots and lowered herself into the swirling water, which came to her armpits and almost took her breath away at first. She regained her balance and made her way under the bridge towards the open bays. Suddenly her feet slipped on a rounded stone in the river-bed and in she plunged. The water gushed into her ears and mouth, but as she stumbled the rope tightened and pulled her to her feet. As the

Guides called out, Lyn heard a whistle. It was faint, but certainly a whistle. Unfortunately, the wind made it difficult to place just where the sound was coming from.

Lyn went on, groping her way through the bridge, holding on to the grey-green, moss-covered wall until she reached the end and could see on to the beach. She stopped to catch her breath, and then she called out. She heard the whistle again, and looking to her right saw two figures huddled together, with the sea surging round their knees.

With Jill in the rope, Lyn worked her way back up the river

She made her way towards them, slowly and carefully, hoping the rope would stretch enough to enable her to reach the figures.

"Come on, Enid!" she called. "Pass Jill over to me quickly, and I'll take her back to the others. Can you hold on until I come back for you? I'll be as quick as I can."

"Oh, Lyn, I've been such a fool," Enid started to say, but Lyn interrupted her.

"Don't let's talk now. Jill looks about all-in."

Lyn took the shivering Jill down into the river beside her. Looping the rope around her as well as herself, she gradually worked her way back up the river towards the rest of the Patrol. By this time the Squire and his groom had arrived and they pulled the two girls out. The groom insisted on going back for Enid. The others started back to camp with Jill and Lyn, while Miss Murphy waited for Enid.

After Enid and Jill had been given a good towelling down and a hot drink, they were put to bed. They seemed to have suffered no serious harm.

Miss Murphy decided to keep Jill in her tent. When she went along to see a very shamefaced Enid, she found Enid did not need to learn the reason why Lyn had decided not to go by the beach; she already knew. Enid now realised that a P.L. cannot always make a popular decision, but must make arrangements into which even the weakest member of a Patrol can fit.

It was a very different Enid who sat up in her sleeping-bag to greet her Patrol when they visited her later that evening.

"I'm sorry about everything," she murmured. "How is Jill?"

"Jill is fine. Don't worry about her, Enid," Isla replied. "She is staying in Miss Murphy's tent tonight; she refuses to go home. She sent you a message. She says you must teach her some more knots."

Enid smiled. Her eyes met Lyn's. The weekend would mean more to the Daffodil Patrol than being the weekend when Lyn gained her Permit.

Enid and Jill were given a good towelling down

15

Make Yourself a Waterproof Cape and Hat

L. Baker Tells You How

Buy a large plastic bag of the thicker type with inverted or folded-in sides.

Carefully cut a hole in it for your head and one for each arm. Turning in a little of the bag, stick a narrow hem around these openings.

You now have a sound waterproof covering that will help to keep you warm and dry. Your arms can be kept inside the bag when not in use.

A Foil Hat Too

For a makeshift waterproof hat, beg or borrow a piece of cooking-foil and fashion it into the style of your choice.

Son Las Doce Y Quarto

This is an attractive way of serving salad. The name is Spanish and means "It is quarter past twelve."

You will need 3 hard-boiled eggs, 1 tube of cheese-spread, 1 carton of Spanish salad, lettuce, cucumber, and any other salad vegetables.

Slice each of the hard-boiled eggs into four and arrange them in a circle round the edge of a serving plate. Use the tube of cheese-spread to pipe the numbers from one to twelve on them, as on a clock face.

Wash the lettuce and arrange it in the centre of the plate so that it forms a dish shape. Pour into this the Spanish salad.

Peel the cucumber, saving two long strips of peel. Prepare the other salad vegetables and arrange them neatly to decorate the clock face.

Make the two hands of the clock from the strips of cucumber and lay them gently on top, pointing to a quarter past twelve. —M.G.P.

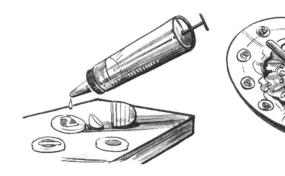

What's Cooking?

Bake potatoes in a different way

When baking potatoes in your camp-fire, make them look and taste different this way: bore a hole through each potato the long way. Into each hole insert a sausage.

Wrap the lot in foil before putting it into the fire to bake. In this way sausage and potato are cooked at the same time, and flavour is added to the potato. —L.B.

16

Painting the Seasons

by Marcia M. Armitage

Colour the springtime pink and see
 The blossom appear on the almond tree,
While puffs of cloud go floating by
 Like candyfloss in the evening sky.

Colour the summer blue to make
 A kingfisher flash across the lake.
Delphiniums, cornflowers, lupins too,
 Reflect a sky of brilliant blue.

Colour the autumn burnished gold
 For shaggy chrysanthemums to unfold;
And scuffling leaves of orange and brown
 Through the misty days come tumbling down.

Colour the winter red as flames
 Like the children's cheeks in their tingling games.
A frosty sun casts a rosy glow
 Over the crackling ice and snow.

Colour each season with great care,
 And you will see appearing there
A picture set in Nature's frame,
 For this is her own colouring game.

Colour slide by Alan Band Associates

Over seven hundred years ago, at the end of a day's fighting, King Waldemar the Victorious, of Denmark, glanced wearily up at the sky and saw to his amazement a huge white cross set against the red background of the sunset. This he took as a sign from heaven, so the tale goes, that he would win his next battle. Filled with renewed strength, he did just that.

So in 1219 Denmark adopted the white cross on a red background for their flag, which is

ROFLAGS

called the Dannebrog, the "Strength of Denmark", and the same design has been used ever since.

Of the nine nations comprising the European Economic Community, or Common Market, Denmark is the only one to keep the same flag for nearly a thousand years.

Flags are so old that nobody knows who invented them, but we do know they are mentioned in the Bible and that they were used by all the ancient peoples.

The earliest English flag at sea as well as on land was probably the Golden Dragon of Wessex, under which the English forces warred against the Danes. But the first Union Flag did not appear until 1606, after James VI of Scotland had become James I of England. Then neither the English nor the Scots wel-

comed it, and during the Commonwealth it went out of use but was flown again at the Restoration and remained unchanged for many years.

In 1801 the flag was altered to symbolize the United Kingdom of Great Britain and Ireland. As every Guide knows, the flag is made up of three crosses: the red cross of St. George of England, the white diagonal cross of St. Andrew of Scotland, and the red diagonal cross of St. Patrick of Ireland.

The people of Eire fly their own national flag, a tricolour of green, white and orange, often referred to as "the green, white and gold".

When William of Orange freed Holland from the rule of the Spanish he flew the colours of orange, white and blue. This Prinsevlag, as it was called, is still flown on some special occasion, but the orange stripe on the official flag of the Netherlands has been changed to red.

Before the introduction of the present tricolour, France did not have a national flag. Various great families had their own standards and pennants, but there was nothing for the whole nation. Many years before the revolution, the royal standard was a white flag with gold fleur-de-lys, but this gave way to a three-colour flag of blue, white and red similar to the present tricolour.

During the German occupation of France the Free French led by General de Gaulle had their own tricolour, which bore on its white stripe a red emblem, the Cross of Lorraine.

Many revolutionary countries have adopted the tricolour—a flag with three stripes—as their national emblem, this being the sign of a successful revolution. The national flag of Italy, for instance, is a vertical tricolour of green, white and red.

Belgium's flag is also a vertical tricolour of black, yellow and red. It was originally a revolutionary flag, for the Belgians revolted against the Hapsburgs and rallied under the flag of Brabant, and this revolt gave its name to the Belgian national anthem, the *Branbançonne.*

The Grand Duchy of Luxembourg flies a horizontal tricolour similar to that of the Netherlands, but it is shorter and its colours are taken from the Duchy's coat-of-arms, which are red, white and light-blue.

In the days of the German empire the Imperial Arms were an eagle, while the national flag was black, white and red, but when the empire fell after World War I the new flag was a tricolour of black, red and gold. The Nazi government abolished this flag, replacing it by one of their own, a red flag with a large white circle in the centre containing the black swastika emblem. Germany is now divided into two independent nations. One of them, the German Federal Republic of West Germany, has restored the former emblem of the eagle, and the horizontal colours of the flag are black, red and gold.

These then are the flags of the nine Common Market countries.

19

These are the Flags of the Nine Common Market Countries

United Kingdom

Holland

Denmark

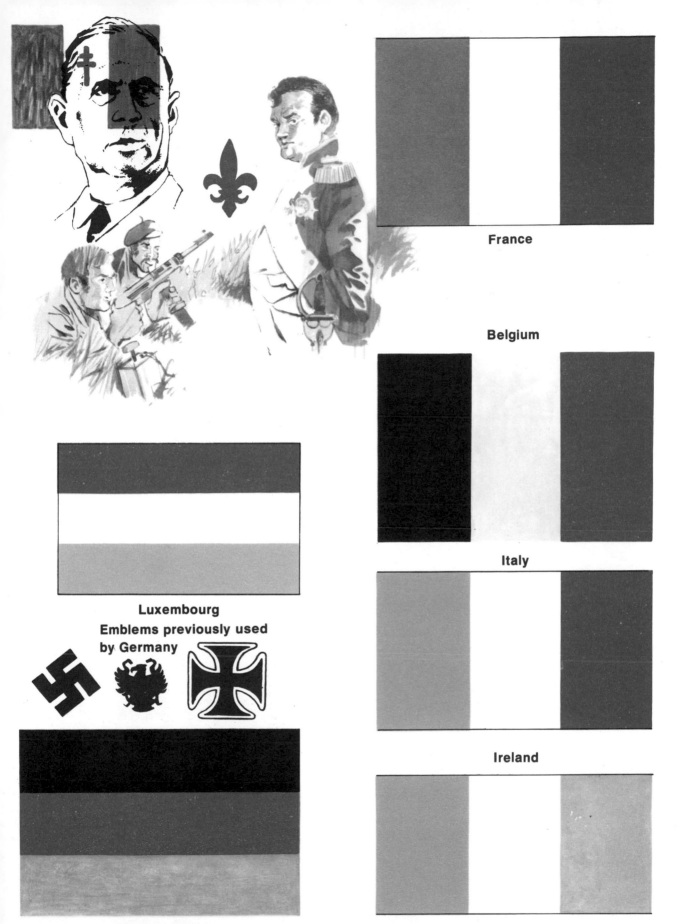

France

Belgium

Italy

Ireland

Luxembourg

Emblems previously used
by Germany

West Germany

21

It's fast, it's exciting, it's safe~ It's Grass Skiing

Jane Monro Tells You About It

Photographs and colour slides by Ski Club of Great Britain

Grass-skiers on Box Hill, Surrey

If you've seen people apparently skiing down grassy hillsides your eyes have not been deceiving you: they were grass skiing. The sport has become increasingly popular since it first appeared in England five years ago, and as the equipment has been vastly improved so grass skiing has become more exciting.

There are two types of ski, and the first one appeared as long ago as 1963; a German knitting-machine manufacturer was determined to devise some method of skiing on grass. Although various efforts had already been made by other people, none had succeeded. The prototype, which has remained the basis of the Rollka grass ski ever since, consists of a caterpillar track running round a metal frame, and it moves rather like a tank. The original skis were less than fifteen inches long, but they proved rather too small and insubstantial, and indeed a number of would-be grass skiers were thoroughly put off the whole idea! So the inventor continued to experiment, and about four years ago he produced a longer and broader ski which made a marked difference to the sport. Since the introduction of the "maxi" and then the "jumbo", which is thirty inches long, the sport has taken on a new lease of life, and fast skiers now travel at speeds up to 40 mph.

Three years ago there was another breakthrough. An Englishman invented a grass ski. Called the Grilson grass skis, these are of a simpler design, comprising five rollers under a metal box frame. Although racers still prefer the Rollkas, Grilsons are ideal for learning on and most recreational skiers prefer this type, finding them more stable and therefore better for their confidence. Another point in their favour is that they are cheaper than Rollkas, which have to be imported from Germany. Rollkas cost between £35 and £40 a pair, Grilsons between £25 and £30.

The most important part of the equipment for snow skiing is a good pair of boots, and this is also true for grass skiing. The foot is three or four inches above the ground, so the ankle needs support, and as the knees do the work, pushing the skis round turns, stiff boots are a help. You want sticks too; ordinary ski sticks are fine as long as corks or something are fixed over the points to prevent them from sticking in the ground while you go on! And broom poles do very well too, if they're cut to the right length.

You'll have realised that grass skis are quite different from snow skis, and they move differently because they don't slide sidewards as a ski can on snow. Yet the sensation is very similar and all the thrills and speed are there. And there's a major advantage which you'll appreciate if you've had the chance to ski on snow (or an artificial slope). On grass you ski with your skis parallel and never stem or snowplough; this means that you learn to ski with your feet together right from the start, instead of mastering the art of skiing with tips together and feet apart and then changing the method, trying to keep the feet together. There is now a recognised system of instruction organised by the Ski Club of Great Britain—which runs weekly meetings throughout the summer so that people can come along and hire all the equipment and take part in lessons. And this leads to another plus factor, which is that grass skiing is easy to pick up. Certainly snow skiers take to it very quickly indeed, but even those who've never been near snow do acquire the feel of it in a very short time. Most beginners who have a lesson and then practise for an afternoon are competent to take part in an easy race at the end of the day.

Competitions and races are often run on a handicap system, so the best skiers don't

An expert grass skier executes a royale—a turn with one ski out to the side

"Ski-joring" behind a car at Petersfield, Hampshire

At a meeting in France two racers start off on a parallel slalom

Seven grass-skiers prepare for the "off" on a trans-Pennine track above Edale, Derbyshire

Viktor Strefling, Bavarian snow-ski champion and winner of an international grass-skiing meeting in England, "in the air"

necessarily win. **They can take part in the National Championship Races and collect points during the season, the winner being the skier with the best four results.**

Naturally these races attract a lot of entries and they also prove very entertaining for spectators. Some of the falls and spills look highly spectacular, but the short skis mean that legs don't get broken and injuries are generally restricted to bruises and muddy jeans. The most exciting races are the team parallel slaloms, in which two teams of four race each other down parallel courses; being able to see who is winning obviously makes it all the more tense, and those watching get very partisan about particular teams. Several Ranger and Venture Scout Units have bought themselves skis, and we're getting hot competition from them—and hope that there will shorty be several Scout and Guide teams taking part.

Racers may like to climb up the hill to get fit, but others make full use of the lift the Ski Club provides, preferring to save their energy for the downhill work—especially if it's a steep slope, and really good steep slopes are few and far between. Turfy terrain, such as downland, is excellent, but it's better to avoid the areas recently grazed by sheep and cows since only good skiers

are probably adept enough to avoid the cowpats. It's also important to ascertain who owns the land and to ask permission to use it before setting off with whoops of delight down a field of newly grown wheat.

Then, rather than keeping to one slope, you can go trekking. To launch one season the Ski Club of Great Britain did a Trans-Pennine Grass Ski Trek from Macclesfield to Cheshire, covering about thirty miles of very varied countryside, and camping *en route* for one night. The television and press were intrigued by it all, as were the bystanders along the route. So the following year we followed up this success with a South Downs "trot"—not quite so arduous because there are no drystone walls and therefore we didn't have to carry ladders to negotiate such hazards (and they can be quite treacherous in ski boots). You can get up quite a speed "langlaufing" along the flat—which the Norwegians do when they ski across country. Indeed, the British Army's Biathalon team has included grass skiing as part of their training for some time now. Undoubtedly

there is a lot of scope for those who want to explore on grass skis, and even if a lot of the ground is unsuitable it's more than gratifying when you discover a good hill and really let go.

So, once you've got the essential equipment and establish a good site, you're well set up, and you might well consider starting up your own local club. The Ski Club of Great Britain, which runs the sport in this country, is always willing to support any such venture, and qualified instructors will come along and give advice. If you would like any help or information the Grass Ski Secretary at the Ski Club, 118 Eaton Square, London, S.W.1, will be delighted to do everything possible for you. Membership fees for country members or the under-25's is less than £4 for the London and district members, and less than £3 for country members.

The only problem with grass skiing is that once you take it up you become addicted to it. So be warned!

***A companionable run down
a slope of Box Hill***

Guiding on a Volcanic Isle

by Barbara Bennett

Handicapped Rangers exhibit their handiwork

There are nearly 1,000 guides on Mauritius, a little sugar-growing island in the Indian Ocean, halfway across the world to Australia. They are not all English Guides, for in Mauritius many different races make their homes. If you visited the island you would see more Chinese, French, Hindu and Creole Guides than English. In fact, there is only one Company of English Guides, and they celebrated their 21st birthday in 1974.

Mauritian Guide and Ranger meetings are always held on a Saturday afternoon. This is because girls are never allowed out at night alone; even if they go to catch a bus they must be accompanied by a male relative.

When all the island Guide Companies meet together for a rally they usually speak French, so unless the English Guides have tried hard at their schoolwork they are a bit stuck as to what is going on! The ordinary people of Mauritius speak a language called Creole, which is a simplified sort of French—with only the present tense used!

The island Guide Companies are not wealthy. They have to raise money to buy their equipment. When one Guide Company needed some tents for camping, they had a very good money-making idea. Every Sunday for more than a year they were at the local church hall from 7.30 a.m. to 11.30 a.m. serving drinks and cakes to the congregations coming from the Roman Catholic masses. The Patrols took it in turns to make the cakes, and there was great competition to see which Patrol raised the most money each week.

Mauritius is a beautiful tropical island where dark-skinned children play on white beaches, where weird-shaped volcanic mountains rise starkly, and where the fifteen-foot-high sugar-cane sways in the warm trade winds. The coral reef which surrounds most of the island makes the beaches safe for bathing, as large, dangerous fish like sharks rarely get through the reef. When the Guides go camping on the warm beaches, however, they wear shoes for swimming, because under the surface lurk such dangers as deadly stone fish, sea-urchins with long, sharp spines, and

Mauritius Guides enjoy a game of basketball

27

Two Mauritius Guides with a Hindu woman and her son, who have collected grass for their cow

Volcanic mountains of weird shapes rise starkly above the sugar-cane

Dark - skinned children play on the white beaches

The white line of the coral-reef shows beyond the forest

Guides of Mauritius cycle in the sunshine through the sugar-cane

stinging geography cones, to mention a few. Nevertheless, many Guides love to snorkel in the clear waters and look at the brightly coloured fish below.

One time of year when it is not advisable to camp is during the cyclone season. This extends from November to March, which is summer-time in Mauritius and very hot. These cyclone winds can rise to 120 m.p.h. in a few minutes and destroy all in their path. Cyclones are always given girls' names; the worst one in recent years was Cyclone Gervaise. In a few hours it destroyed the Island's sugar crop and wrecked homes. The rain which followed washed away many of the straw huts in which the poor people lived. Even on a tropical island one gets weather problems!

There are plenty of things the Guides can do for their Service Flash. Some Guides make toys for the children in the poor villages of straw huts. Others distribute clothes, because many children have only one dress to wear all the year round.

One exciting job which the Guides share with the Scouts is on the occasion of a royal visit. With the police, they line the route and keep back the crowds as the royal party goes by; they get a good view! The Queen and the Duke of Edinburgh and Princess Margaret have visited

the island, and, more recently, Princess Alexandra.

There is one Unit for handicapped Land Rangers in Mauritius. These crippled girls live in a special home. Although they are not all orphans, they rarely if ever see their families, because there is no transport for visiting. Badly crippled as they are, they do not complain. To raise money they do attractive and colourful needlework. When there is a Guide rally, a bus is organised to take the Rangers and their wheel-chairs or crutches, and off they go, singing all the way there and back. Perhaps the most unusual outing they have had was when they were taken on a trip round a visiting Royal Navy ship. The British sailors made a great fuss of them and even organised a ride around the harbour in a boat. For this the girls had to put aside their crutches and, amidst much giggling, be lowered over the side of the ship by a crane hoist!

Guiding is a wonderful thing for the girls of Mauritius, because many of them have to leave school at the early age of twelve. Education is free up to twelve, then the parents have to pay a small amount each term. But if your father is out of work, as many fathers here are, there is no money for such luxuries as education. These girls may get jobs as maids, and eventually

Handicapped Rangers enjoy being hoisted aboard a visiting Royal Navy vessel

earn about £7 a month. They may train as "sewing girls" and take on dressmaking jobs. Nearly all clothes are hand-made. There are no exciting stores displaying the latest fashions. The clever girls train as nurses, and each year, out of hundreds of applicants, a handful are accepted for jobs in England. As they speak French fluently, a few others obtain jobs in France as telephonists, maids or dressmakers.

Every Guide loves a wedding, and in Mauritius even the poorest people put themselves into debt for years for their weddings. These always take place in the early evening. After the religious ceremony, the lady guests go home and change into long evening dresses. Then they return to the wedding party, which is usually a dance and buffet. It is quite usual to see as many as four hundred guests at a wedding, and everyone, including the bride and groom, makes merry till the early hours!

Different as their life is from yours, these girls all belong to the same world-wide Guide Movement. On Thinking Day they may not be polishing up their pennies, but they will be polishing up their rupees and cents with just as much enthusiasm as you do to give to the same World Association.

Handicapped Rangers at a Guide rally

MAKE YOUR OWN DRINKS

A. COOPER Tells You How to Make GINGER POP

You will need to set up what is called a ginger-pop "plant", because the pop grows and grows. Don't worry! You can throw it away (or give it away) if it gets out of hand! All you need is yeast, sugar, ginger, lemons and water.

To begin: Mix 2 ounces (56 grams) of baker's yeast with 2 level tablespoons of sugar until they turn to a liquid. Then add 2 level tablespoons of ground ginger and half a pint (10 fluid ozs) of water.

Put this mixture in a jar and cover it with a *loose* lid. That's all you do on the first day.

Every day for nine days add one level teaspoon of ginger and one level teaspoon of sugar. Stir and re-cover.

On the tenth day you make your ginger pop.

Dissolve 18 ounces of sugar in 1½ pints (30 fluid ozs) of water, bring to the boil and cool slightly. Add to this the strained juice of two lemons.

Strain the plant from the covered jar through a piece of fine material. Keep what is left behind to start a new plant. Add the juice from it to the lemon, sugar and water.

Add 6 pints (3·409 litres) of water and stir.

Bottle in *strong* screw-topped bottles and store in a cool place until you feel thirsty, then drink.

To make more. Put half of the plant (what was left in the straining-cloth) into one jar, and half into another. Work through the recipe again with each jar, leaving out the yeast in the first stage.

Ginger pop

Lemon Syrup

M.G. PEARSON Tells You How to Make this Cool, Refreshing Drink

You can make this in quantity, if you like, and sell it at your next fund-raising bazaar or jumble sale.

To make about three squash-bottles full you need 3 lemons, 2lbs of sugar, 1½ pints of boiling water, ¼ pint of cold water, and 1oz. of citric acid, which you can buy at any chemist's.

Use a potato peeler to peel the lemons very thinly without taking off any of the white pith. Put the rind in a large jug. Cut away the white pith and throw it away. Slice the lemons and put them in the jug. Add the sugar. Pour on the boiling water, stir well to dissolve the sugar, cover and leave until the mixture is cold. Dissolve the citric acid in the cold water and add it to the ingredients in the jug. Strain the mixture through a clean cloth, squeezing it tightly so as not to waste any of the juice. Pour into clean bottles. Serve diluted according to taste.

FOR WHEN YOU GO ABROAD

in Holland

The Swiss Alps at Mürren

Countries of the European Economic Community have a common market but no common language and no common currency, so it's useful to learn at least a few greetings, a few phrases and the names of the currency of the country you're visiting.

Here are some ways of saying Good Day or Good Morning in countries in and outside the Common Market.

DENMARK: God Morgan
ESPERANTO: Bonan Tagon
FRANCE: Bonjour
GERMANY: Guten Morgen
ITALY: Buon Giorno
SOVIET UNION: Izdrashviti
YUGOSLAVIA: Dobar Dan

In the United Kingdom the pound is the standard unit of currency. In other countries the unit is as follows:—

AUSTRIA: Schilling
BELGIUM: Franc
BULGARIA: Lev
DENMARK: Krone
FRANCE: Franc
GERMANY (WEST):
Deutsche Mark
GREECE: Drachma
ITALY: Lira
NETHERLANDS: Guilder

NORWAY: Krona
POLAND: Zloty
PORTUGAL: Escudo
SPAIN: Peseta
SWEDEN: Krona
SOVIET UNION: Ruble
SWITZERLAND: Franc

You are probably familiar by now with metric weights and measures, but here's a reminder of what the metre, the litre and the kilogram represent side by side with our imperial stand-ards:—

METRE: 3ft 3ins.
1 CENTIMETRE: 0.394 inch
2.5 CENTIMETRES: 1 inch

LITRE: 1¾ pints
KILOGRAM: 2¼ lbs.

How's Your English Geography?

by J. G. Ranford

The answer to each clue is a well-known town or locality in England. Number of letters is given in brackets.

1. Meal untouched
   in Warwickshire (8)
2. New lock needs it
   in Cornwall (7)
3. Cardplayers do it
   in Kent (4)
4. Bright coloured girl
   in Cornwall (7)
5. Lean sort of flower
   in Lancashire (9)
6. Beloved heavyweight
   in County Durham (10)
7. Ham or cheese
   in Kent (8)
8. Carry on feeding
   in Buckinghamshire (4)
9. Ship's company
   in Cheshire (5)
10. Dogs are always at it
    in the London area of Essex (7)

Pirate Island

by Jean Howard

"All passengers for Istanbul, Bombay and Hongkong, please go to Channel 5."

At last the moment of departure! Nicola picked up her small hand luggage and followed the other passengers out to the giant jet waiting on the tarmac. Soon they were climbing up into the summer sky and leaving the green fields of England behind.

During the journey, Nicola noticed another girl who was also wearing a small Guide badge in the lapel of her jacket. It wasn't long before she made her acquaintance. They discovered that they were both Patrol Leaders and both working for the Queen's Badge. Both Nicola and Karen were flying to join their parents in Hongkong for the summer holidays.

On arrival at Kaitak airport they found they would be living in the same part of the island.

The days that followed were

The days in Hong Kong were full of fun and excitement for Nicola and Karen

filled with fun and excitement: swimming in the warm sea, water ski-ing, exploring the wonderful island, whose teeming population overflowed on to crowded sampans on the waterfront. In the evenings there were beach parties and barbecues, and Nicola made lots of friends. Her favourite companion, however, was Karen.

They were both anxious to make good use of their holiday to gain more experience for their Queen's Guide badge, so they often spent a morning helping in the local hospital, or looking after a neighbour's small children. Each week they visited the local Guide Company and joined in their meetings, where they took part in songs and dances and gained many new ideas for flower arrangements, basket-making and other crafts.

One morning Karen suggested that they might make up a party and take the ferry across to the nearby island of Macao. Soon six of them were on their way, enjoying the welcome sea-breeze. The island was a fantastic hurly-burly of colour and sound, race and language. The narrow, crowded streets made it difficult to keep together, and after a while Nicola and Karen decided to go and explore the old market-place, arranging to meet the others back at the ferry later on in the day.

The sights and sounds and smells were all so strange and exciting that they hardly knew what to look at first. Everywhere was noise and bustle and talk and laughter. There was new food and fruits to try, and exotic perfumes to smell.

The girls wandered on and on, buying a few trinkets here and there and comparing the scene with the orderly shopping centres at home. Gradually, they both became aware of being watched. Uneasy, they began to make their way back towards the main part of the town, but each turning they took led them into narrow, squalid streets.

By now they were sure they were being followed, but when they tried to hurry and push their way through the crowds they received angry glances and sensed a feeling of hostility building up around them.

The girls were sure they were being followed

The labyrinth of streets and passages seemed endless, and the smell from the open drains was almost overpowering. Instead of doors, the shanties had bead

curtains that rustled in the breeze, as if hidden figures were watching them, and scraggy chickens ran squawking from under their hurrying feet. The girls heartily wished they had not ventured so far.

At last they saw the sparkle of the sea ahead and began to run down a narrow lane between some tumbledown shanties — only to find their way blocked by the grime-blackened wall of an old boathouse. A small wooden door that had once been painted blue hung from broken hinges. It offered a means of escape.

"Quick, through there!" gasped Nicola, clutching Karen's arm.

But before they could reach it rough hands grabbed them. They were quickly gagged and blindfolded with pieces of foul-smelling cloth and dragged forward. The door creaked on its rusty hinges as they were pushed through; then the smell of tar and rope and seaweed told them that they were near the water's edge.

Their captors held a hurried conference, and then they felt themselves being pulled up a narrow plank which knocked their feet and ankles as they slipped and stumbled forward.

"Now jump!" rasped a voice.

As they half jumped and half fell down several feet on to some heavy coils of rope below, Karen felt a sharp pain in her wrist as she put her hand back to save herself. They struggled into a sitting position; then they felt a rocking movement and realised they were afloat!

Petrified with fear, they could do nothing but try to grip the ropes and keep their balance. An ancient diesel motor had cranked into life, and the craft moved out into the open sea.

After what seemed hours, the dirty rags were pulled roughly from their faces. At first they were dazzled by the bright sunlight on the water. Gradually, as their eyes became accustomed to the glare, they saw they were in a large Chinese junk, its big, red-brown sails filling out in the fresh breeze.

An evil-looking man, clad in a tattered shirt and pair of shorts, grinned at them and said in broken English, "Welcome, missies, to my

Before they could reach the door rough hands grabbed them

velly humble boat. We go for nice sail to distant island, and we stay there till your fathers pay velly nice lot of money to our good friend Ah Fung in Hongkong!"

Nicola was so angry that she forgot to be frightened. Glaring at the man, she shouted, "How dare you! You're nothing more than a pirate. You won't get away with this, you know."

He only laughed and said she could shout as much as she liked as no one could hear her.

"Don't say any more," whispered Karen. "It will only make things worse."

The man, who seemed to be the captain, shuffled off to speak to some of the crew. Nicola noticed that Karen was holding her wrist.

"What have you done?" she asked softly. "Have you hurt it?"

"I think I sprained it as I fell. Perhaps you could bandage it for me with a bit of that rag; it is swelling up rather."

Nicola managed to bind up the injured arm, and made a sling out of another piece of cloth. She smiled to herself as she realised she had carefully done a reef-knot. The captain had disappeared into a small cabin amidships, and she looked round for somewhere more comfortable for Karen to sit. Near by there was a large box covered by a piece of sailcloth. She tried to pull it nearer, but it was too heavy. Lifting a corner of the cloth, she saw that the box had strong metal hinges and a large padlock. They were discussing what could be inside when Karen happened to glance out to sea. There was a naval patrol-boat passing abreast of them a little distance away.

"Quick—your bag, Nicola!" she whispered, grabbing the satchel that still hung from Nicola's shoulder. "I lost mine in the struggle on the wharf, I think. Ah, here's your powder compact. Look! You can use the mirror in the lid to flash a message."

Opening the compact, Nicola held it facing the patrol-boat, and, catching the sun's rays on the mirror, sent an SOS signal by rapidly opening and shutting the little case: three quick dots, three longer

The girls were hustled down below

dashes, three quick dots again.

Several times she repeated the urgent message. To their joy, the boat altered course towards them.

A cry from one of the crew brought the captain out of the cabin. He quickly realised what was happening. Shouting to the nearest men to help him, he pulled up a hatch cover. The girls were hustled down below. The hatch was slammed shut and something heavy dragged over it. Nicola and Karen lay helpless in the stifling darkness.

The sound of powerful engines grew louder, and then the girls heard someone with an English voice hail the junk and ask whether assistance was needed, as a light had flashed.

"Oh, no! Have no trouble, thank you. Must have been sun on brass bell. Velly fine bell, and mate keep

it velly bright." Craftily the captain pointed to an old ship's bell that swung to and fro with the motion of the craft.

The young officer of the vessel scanned the junk with his binoculars. As there seemed to be nothing amiss, he had to accept the explanation and let the vessel go on its way.

As soon as the patrol-boat was out of sight, the hatch was opened and the girls were pulled back on deck. They were glad to gulp in the fresh air, but were bitterly disappointed that their hopes of rescue had failed. Their situation was as grave as ever.

Their captors became busy setting the sails to make the most of the westerly breeze, and soon the junk was skimming across the water, taking the girls further and further away from home.

The late afternoon sun scorched down from a cloudless sky, and Nicola asked a sailor who was working near her for a drink of water.

He glanced anxiously over his shoulder towards the captain, who was hidden for the moment by the main-sail, then quickly filled a cracked cup from a tub of brackish water and handed it to her. Both girls had a quick drink, though the smell and taste were far from pleasant, and they poured the rest over Karen's swollen wrist.

The sailor had just replaced the cup when the captain came aft and gruffly told them they would soon be reaching the island of Lantao, where they would be kept in hiding until he received a message from Hongkong that the ransom money was paid. With an evil grin he warned them that any attempt at escape would fail and be the worse for them.

The girls could now see a rugged coastline looming up out of the late afternoon haze. After running along it for some distance, the junk altered course to starboard and sailed into a small cove whose entrance was fairly well concealed.

Being well trained in observation, Karen and Nicola watched the coast carefully for distinctive landmarks. A sea mist made visibility poor, but they noticed a small harbour where several grey ships were flying what seemed to be the white ensign. Further inland, they caught a glimpse of a large building with a tower, where a flock of seagulls were wheeling and crying, which suggested a habitation or source of food.

Darkness was beginning to fall as the junk dropped anchor about two hundred yards from the boulder-strewn shore. The captain and several of the crew went ashore in a dinghy. Before leaving, he warned the rest of the men to keep a close watch on the prisoners and with an ugly laugh indicated the long curved knives in their belts.

The girls shivered as the night air became chill, and they huddled together for warmth. The smell of cooking came from the cabin. The man who had given them water

The captain and several of the crew went ashore in a dinghy, leaving the girls prisoners

brought them a small helping of broken-up fish and rice. The chipped enamel plates were far from clean, but they were too hungry to worry about that. After a while their guards settled down to a game of mahjong by the light of a small hurricane lamp in the forepeak, which cast weird shadows on the deck.

"Isn't there something we can do while there are only a few of them?" whispered Nicola.

"We can't just dive overboard and swim for it," replied Karen. "They'd hear us at once and we wouldn't stand a chance."

As she spoke, she moved to ease her aching limbs. A length of rope slipped off the pile and lay on the deck beside them. One of the men looked up sharply at the sound, but seeing they hadn't moved he soon became absorbed in the game again.

The sight of the rope gave Nicola an idea, and in a low whisper she said, "A single rope would be no good because of your wrist, but if we could make a rope-ladder we could lower it over the side, climb down it, and slip into the water."

"It's worth a try," agreed Karen. "Anything is better than just sitting here. We'll have to fold it in half, and then I'll steady it while you tie the knots."

This was something Nicola had often done during night-incident courses or in joint activities with the Scouts. She soon completed several rungs, with neat double-overhands at one end and sheetbends at the other. Afraid that the slightest noise would give them away, they worked slowly, being careful that the rope didn't scrape on the deck. Finally they decided the ladder was long enough.

There was a small iron cleat at the edge of the deck. It was used for the mooring-ropes when the junk was alongside a wharf. It made a good place from which to sling the ladder, which it would hold firm.

Inch by inch the girls crept across the deck, using the dark shadows for cover. Slowly they lowered the ladder over the side, having first made it fast to the cleat. They worked in silence.

"I'll go down first," whispered Nicola. "Then I can steady it while you follow me."

Without a sound, she lowered herself down the ladder and disappeared from view. A gentle tug on the rope gave Karen the signal to follow. Although her wrist was painful, she removed the sling and began the descent. Each time her arms had to take the strain she bit her lip with pain, but she knew the slightest sound would betray them.

Silently Karen followed Nicola down the rope

Slowly she crept down until cold water lapped round her feet.

A few more seconds and both girls were swimming silently towards the shore. Both had their Swimmer and Life Saver badges and had often practised swimming in their clothes.

The moon was just beginning to rise as they reached the shore. They crept carefully up over stones. Any noise would carry on the still night air and perhaps bring their captors after them. For one awful moment Karen thought she had given their presence away. As they reached the tide-line she nearly stepped on a huge shell edged with jagged teeth. Just in time, she muffled a scream and hastily stepped to one side.

"I expect it's a king crab," whispered Nicola.

She led the way towards steep cliffs. Fortunately they found a narrow cleft with a few good footholds. With Nicola's assistance, Karen managed to scramble to the top, where both lay panting on the cool grass.

Karen's arm was throbbing painfully, but they hadn't a moment to lose. From the clifftop, they saw the dinghy returning to the junk. As soon as the captain discovered their absence, he would set off in pursuit.

The early evening mist had cleared, and Nicola was thankful to see the Plough and Cassiopeia twinkling in the heavens. Remembering in which direction the sun had set, they took a bearing on the stars and set off down the coast towards the harbour, where they hoped to reach safety.

The sound of angry cries from the direction of the cove presently told them their flight had been discovered. They hurried over the rough ground, expecting every moment to hear sounds of pursuit. They had gone some distance when a deep inlet forced them to move further inland. It became more and more difficult to find their way. The sky had clouded over, and there was only the moon to help them. In about half an hour they became aware that a huge building had loomed up in front of them. Nicola, who was leading, stopped abruptly and pulled Karen to the ground.

Two men in uniform and carrying rifles were talking in low voices outside an entrance in the high walls. After a few minutes one went inside and the other began to patrol the building. The girls dared not risk being seen in case the men should be unfriendly, so, although their limbs were aching with weariness, they crept

past as soon as he turned the corner, and hurried on.

They dropped down into a valley and groped their way through a thick belt of trees and scrub. The branches stung their faces and arms and they tripped over roots. Feeling utterly exhausted, they began to think they would never reach the harbour and safety. In desperation however, they pushed on until finally they broke through the trees. Before them was the outline of a building. High up in a tower a bell began to toll. A door opened, framing a saffron-robed monk. He paused for a moment, looking into the darkness. The girls cried out for help and staggered towards the monastery gate.

The next few hours were rather hazy, but Karen and Nicola knew they had found safety and kindness at the monastery of Tongfuk. Word was sent from there to the officer in charge of troops guarding

a big reservoir that was a reserve water-supply for Hongkong. Later, a Land Rover took them down to the harbour, where a motor-boat bore them swiftly back to their anxious parents. On the way, they learned that the first building they had seen was a prison, where the guards would have taken them to safety.

A naval patrol-boat was soon on its way to the cove, and within a few hours the pirate captain and his crew were taken into custody. When the junk was searched, guns and ammunition were found in the box they had tried to open. The discovery put the police on to the track of a gunrunning gang.

Karen and Nicola both gained their Queen's Guide badges. They recognised with gratitude that the knowledge and skill they gained through working for the badge had contributed in no small measure to their escape from Pirate Island.

The girls cried out and staggered towards the monk

Weighty Words

by A. L. Blowers

The answers to all these clues contain the word TON.

1 A rating for ships
2 A famous school
3 Refers to pitch and quality
4 Source of communication
5 Lifting aid
6 Invigorating
7 Cotton or linen fabric
8 Piece of rock
9 Famous cookery book author
10 Creeping rockery plant
11 Famous poet
12 English cheese
13 Popular writer of children's books
14 A famous palace
15 A bird
16 Well-known suspension bridge
17 To make amends
18 Prehistoric stone monument
19 Recite in a singing voice

Guess the Wildflower

by Daphne M. Pilcher

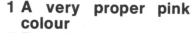

1 A very proper pink colour
2 Female ox in a position on the cricket pitch
3 Rabbit-like animal that rings
4 Bushy-tailed animal that must have a hand
5 Spread on your bread and then drunk from
6 Reddish-brown coloured horse
7 Used to sweep the floor
8 Part of the eye
9 The last colour of the rainbow
10 To sew an ugly growth
11 Economy
12 Christmas bird in tatters
13 Emblem of Scotland
14 Never forget
15 Wet big black bird of twelve inches

Foam Fish

Either as a gift or to sell on a stall, soap is always pleasing. Try making this foam fish so that it is more attractive than the average soap gift.

You will need sufficient foam to cur out two fish shapes twice the size of the template shown. Don't use too thin foam or it won't sew satisfactorily; on the other hand, too thick will be unmanageable.

Draw the outline of the fish on the foam (ballpoint lines show better than pencil) twice, then cut out. Cutting out with pinking shears makes the finished article more attractive.

Put the two shapes together and chain-stitch them along the dotted line.

Using the pinking shears, cut along the tail lines. Then all you need do is to pop a cake of soap inside.
—D.M.P.

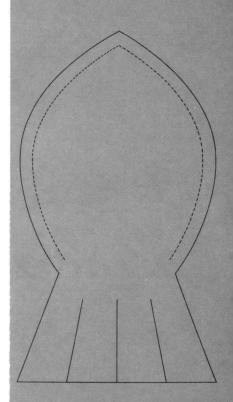

42

Things to make for the Craft Badge

A great variety of things can be made to qualify for the Craft Badge. Here are one or two suggestions for simple but effective articles.

A Feather Brooch

Here is a way of using feathers collected on country walks. If you have none already, you can probably beg some small chicken feathers from a butcher.

You will need about 15 small feathers, a small circle of thin card (to obtain which draw round a 1p piece), a small "gold" safety-pin, a bead or shanked button, needle and thread, glue.

Arrange the feathers in a circle on the card so that the ends meet in the centre. Overlap them slightly, so that there are no gaps. Stick them in place with the glue and leave until dry.

Now position the safety-pin on the back of the card and stitch it firmly in place. Do not fasten off. Instead, bring the needle through to the front, thread the button or bead on to it and sew down in the centre of the card so that all untidy ends and loose stitches are hidden. **—M.G.P.**

Wall Plaque

An attractive wall-plaque can be made from an assortment of ordinary marbles and the inside container of a box of chocolates. These boxes come in various patterns, but some light-silver or gold-coloured ones are in chocolate liqueur boxes.

The container I used contained sixteen liqueurs, so I needed sixteen marbles.

First, I decided on the colour and design I wanted to make with my marbles.

I put a little Evo Stik into each hole, taking care not to allow it to drip anywhere else. Bostik or any other contact adhesive would do equally well. I did not find it necessary to coat the marble with adhesive, although the makers recommend this.

I pressed each marble into its chosen place and let it dry overnight.

I backed the plaque. As the liqueurs came in a wooden box, the lid of the box was exactly the right size. If your box is cardboard, a really stiff piece would do equally well. Following the makers' instructions this time, I applied adhesive to the back of my plaque and the wood and cardboard to which I wanted to attach it. Allowing it to dry slightly, I pressed firmly together and left it to dry overnight.

In order to hang it, I took two large drawing-pins. The kind with coloured heads look well, but the ordinary kind are quite suitable. Cutting a small piece of ribbon or tape, I pushed a drawing-pin through each end and formed a loop for hanging the plaque. On a cardboard backing, the loop could be made by sticking the ribbon or tape in place with contact adhesive.

If placed in a sunny position, the foil and marbles catch the light, and the whole effect is very attractive. **L.B.**

The Story Behind the Field~Name

**How Did "Barebones" or "Farthing Field" Get Its Strange Name?
P. THOMPSON Tells You How and Suggests a Project for Local History Badge**

Are you camping in "Australia" this year? Very unlikely, unless that happens to be the name of the field where you pitch your tents. If it is a long way from the farmhouse, it may even be called "North Pole" or "Moon Ground" on account of its remoteness!

Most fields on a farm have names, but you will not be able to find them on an ordinary Ordnance Survey map, although they are written in on old tithe-maps, which you can usually find at a County Records Office. Each field has a reference number used for Ministry of Agriculture returns and other forms by the farmer. But he will tell his men to go ploughing in "Crosslands" or cutting hay on "Strawberry Hill", not in 535 or 662!

Small fields near the buildings are often called "Close", "Croft" or "Garth". The last is a Norse word meaning an enclosure. This is a reminder of Scandinavian invaders of England many centuries ago. Other relics of their language are "keld", meaning spring, "fell" for hill, "gill" for valley, and "wath" instead of ford. So these are clues that help you discover why a field has acquired a particular name.

The origin of it is not always as obvious as it appears, however. Each successive farmer probably puts a piece of land to a different use; we no longer keep pigs on our farm, so "Pig Mead" has become known as "Sam's Field", Sam being the name of a favourite horse that used to live in that meadow. We also have a "Thomas Close", but have no idea who Thomas was!

The name or occupation of the owner often did get attached to a field — "Barber's Furlong" or "Constable's Paddock", for instance. A furlong was an area of ten acres, and many fields are called after their size or their shape — "Leg of Mutton", "Star", "Hundred Acres". "Bride's Field" may mean that this was part of a girl's marriage dowry.

The Church often owned land in or around a village. "Glebelands" is probably ground that the clergyman took over when he became parson of the place. Not many of the clergy farm now, but it used to be the custom for them to do so as well as carrying out their church duties. This was really a good idea, as they then had much in common with the people of an agricultural community. "Canon's Field" or "Vicar's" may also refer to glebeland, but "Little Heaven", "Golden Field" or "Butter Field" usually meant that this was a very fertile spot, capable of growing good crops. In contrast, "Barebones" or "Starvecrow" are likely to be an unprofitable part of the farm.

Rents paid long ago certainly seem to have been a great deal less than those today. "Sixpenny Bit", "Shilling Ground" and even "Farthing Field" are names that occur.

Flat, level fields near a river or stream were often called "Hams" in the south-west of England. "Pawlett Hams" in Somerset and the South Devon Hams are good cattle-grazing areas.

In Tudor times, everyone had to attend church on Sunday morning or else pay a fine. On Sunday afternoon the men and boys of the

Are you camping this year in Australia or the North Pole?

Photo by Mrs. B. Pescod

Perhaps your camp will give the name "Camp Field", "Guides' Field", or "Campers' Wood" to a site

village often used to practise with the longbow, as it was compulsory for them to do this at least once a week. In fact, to prevent the neglect of archery, legislation in the six-teenth century forbade bowls and football! And so we still have fields called "Butts", where archery prac-tice used to take place. Such a field will often be found to face a large bank or steep hill, for obvious reasons.

Sometimes a landowner left fields to the parish in his will; these were to be let to provide money for the poor and needy. Our West Country village school still receives money in this way under the 1725 will of a Master of Queen's College, Cambridge, and our Vicar has to approve how it is spent. The name "Poorlands" recalls such a gift.

The word "threap" means an argument in northern dialect, so

if you find that a field called "Threapland" is near a parish boundary you may be certain it was once involved in a dispute as to which parish it lay in.

There are many more interesting facts to be learned from field names. "Lord's Park" is likely to have been a deer-park previously; the large hollows in a field called "Canals" or "Vivary" were prob-ably once fishponds belonging to a nearby monastery or nunnery; the local gallows were on "Gallows Hill". In Nottinghamshire, there is even a field called "Candle Rush Car", where rushes were grown in the days when they were used to make lights. But that field is prob-ably rather damp for camping!

Try to find out the name of the field you camp in. Its origin might be a splendid subject for a camp-fire entertainment, although it is advisable not to try hanging some-

one if you should be on Gibbet Hill!

Finding out the origin of six local place-names, as required for part of the Local History badge, might include research into field-names, and in the process you might unearth some surprising facts.

Local History Badge

45

Funfare

A mother sardine and her small offspring were swimming in the sea when a submarine passed by.

"Don't be scared," the mother told her youngsters. "It's only a can of people."

They had been in camp several days when Fiona developed a temperature. She was put in the sick tent, and her P.L. was sent to the doctor with a message: "Please attend our camp as soon as possible. We have a girl with a temperature of 120." Back came the reply: "You don't need me. Send for a fire-engine."

The farmer had fenced off a dangerous spot near the edge of a cliff near the Guides' campsite. A Guide asked him: "Is the cliff very high?"

"Oh, yes, about two hundred feet," replied the farmer.

"That's very high. Do people fall over it very often?"

"No — only once."

P.L.: "I don't know what my Second does with all her money."
Guide: "Why, was she trying to borrow from you?"
P.L.: "No, I was trying to borrow from her."

Guide: "I'm sorry, conductor; my dog has eaten my ticket."
Conductor: "Then you'll have to buy him a second helping, won't you?"

Eager to outdo a rival, a film star paid a thousand pounds for a mynah bird, which he sent to his lady-love for Christmas. The bird could speak in three languages, sing grand opera and recite poetry. Filming on location on Christmas Day, he put through a long-distance call in the evening.

"Did you like the bird, darling?" he asked.

"It was delicious," she replied.

The polite young Guide heard that the Guider was leaving. "I hear we are to have the pleasure of losing you," she said.

P.L.: "What picture do you like best on your TV, Cynthia?"
Cynthia: "I think the one of my brother."

The same young Guide excelled herself when the District Commissioner, testing the Company's Guiding knowledge, asked if any of them knew who the mother of Baden-Powell was. No one knew, except the youngest Guide, who piped up, "Mrs Powell."

"There's isn't a telephone in this one"

A young Guide came home from Company meeting and told her parents that she wanted to take a contribution the following week for the Guider.

"Why, what's it for?" they asked.

"She's leaving and the Guides want to give her a little momentum."

Mandy was carrying the milk pudding at camp when she tripped over a log and spilt the lot.

"That was lucky," she said.

"Lucky?" cried her P.L. "What's lucky about spilling the milk pudding and leaving us without a sweet after our meat?"

"It's lucky because I don't like milk pudding."

Denise: "I'm going to bring a bucket in and let you kick it, Grandpa."
Grandpa: "What in the world for?"
Denise: "I heard Dad and Mum say that we shall get a lot of money when you kick the bucket."

Jokes

What makes a Guide?

Asks Marcia M. Armitage

Is it trying to be helpful when you feel like sitting down?
Is it putting on a cheerful face when you'd really rather frown?
Is it holding on to temper when you're tempted to let fly?
Is it doing what you're told to do without the question why?
Is it sharing your possessions, pushing selfish thoughts aside?
Yes, it's all these things and more that make a girl into a Guide.

Guide Lines

Personal ambition is apt to give you either a swelled head or a soured mind, according as it is fulfilled or foiled.

Usefulness is the rent we pay for living on the earth.

It's not enough to say,
"I'm sorry" and repent,
And then to go on afterwards
Just as you always went.

A good beginning and a good ending make a good speech—if they come close enough together.

Kindness is a language that the deaf can hear and the blind can read.

The ladder of success cannot be climbed with hands in pockets.

When success turns your head you are facing failure.

Nature hath no blemish but the mind;
None can be called deformed but the unkind.

Be Prepared and don't be scared
By difficult work or play.
To fry an egg or mend a leg
Is all in the work of the day.

Isn't it strange that princes and kings
And clowns that caper in sawdust rings
And ordinary folk like you and me
Are builders of eternity?
To each is given a bag of tools,
An hour-glass and a book of rules,
And each must build ere his life is flown
A stumbling block or a stepping stone.

Time to do well, time to do better;
Give up that grudge, answer that letter.
Speak that kind word to sweeten that sorrow;
Do that kind deed you would leave till tomorrow.

Few of us get dizzy from doing too many good turns.

Build castles in the air—but put foundations under them.

He who is not contented with what he has would not be contented with what he would like to have.

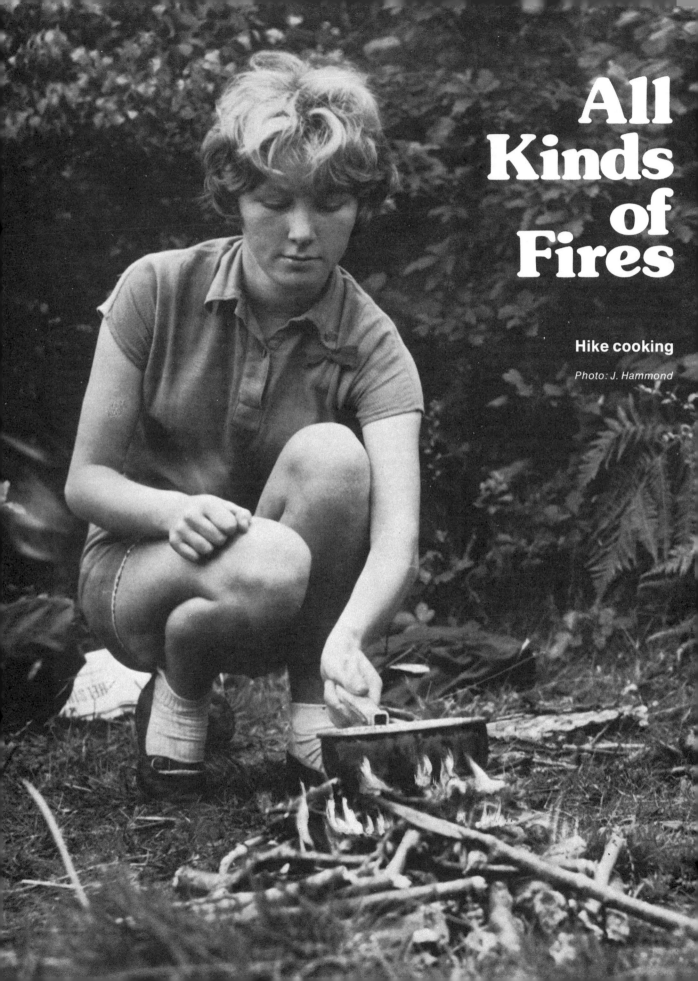

All Kinds of Fires

Hike cooking

Photo: J. Hammond

Altar-fires—
with a difference

One P.L. left a large gap at the base big enough to take a biscuit-tin oven and the necessary fire beneath it. So two types of cooking were possible in one fire, each completely separate from the other.

Another Guide built an altar-fire against a drystone wall, after getting permission from the farmer-owner. The fire had several advantages. The wind, as it blew over the top of the wall, acted as a chimney and drew the fire up. In addition, in the gaps in the wall the Guide stuck sticks, which acted as supports to her billies. Lastly, by making the fire-bed slope very slightly downward towards the wall, the resourceful Guide ensured that the cooking-pots couldn't slide off the fire to the ground; they merely came to rest against the wall.

The Star or Lazyman's. This is good when you want a small fire that will last a long time. It is easy to stoke by just pushing in the star logs as they burn.

The Tramper's. This is a splendid fire for cooking on. Build several little pyramids. When they are burning well, stoke by pushing long pieces of wood along the length of the fire. Use green logs for the outside limiting pieces and for the crosspieces that support your cooking-pots.

How many varieties of fire do you know? It's useful to know which are easiest and quickest to build, which lasts longest and needs least attention, and so on. Here are a few worth knowing about.

The Cobhouse. This makes a grand blaze for a camp sing-song. The effectiveness of it depends upon its little central pyramid. Build the square "cobhouse" with good big pieces of wood.

The Pyramid. This is the basis of all fires. The secret is to take great pains in building the central part, using really small, dry kindling that lights easily.

The Story of the Salvation Army

by Gary Keane and Neville Randall

GENERAL NO.1, WILLIAM BOOTH. WHO SOUGHT OUT THE DREGS AND OUTCASTS OF SOCIETY. AND ENROLLED THEM IN AN ARMY THAT MARCHED ROUND THE WORLD — TO FIGHT FOR GOD.

HE WILL FIGHT HUNGER, HOMELESSNESS AND DESPAIR. ARMED WITH SOUP, SYMPATHY AND BRASS BANDS. PROVIDE SHELTER AND HOPE FOR UNMARRIED MOTHERS, CRIMINALS, PROSTITUTES, ALCOHOLICS AND INTENDING SUICIDES.

1865. LONDON'S EAST END. SEWERS EMPTIED DIRECT INTO THE THAMES. EVERY FIFTH SHOP SOLD GIN. STARVING CHILDREN DRANK IT AT 1d. A GLASS. AND DIED OF CIRRHOSIS OF THE LIVER.

AN EVENING IN JUNE. WHITECHAPEL. OUTSIDE THE BLIND BEGGAR PUB, A PAVEMENT MISSION MEETING WAS ENDING. A 6FT. 1IN. STRANGER STEPPED FORWARD TO SPEAK.

HIS NAME: WILLIAM BOOTH. 36. FATHER OF SIX. DISSENTING METHODIST MINISTER.

THE MISSION'S LEADER WAS SICK. BOOTH WAS ASKED TO HELP. DISCUSSED IT WITH CATHERINE, HIS WIFE.

"WHERE CAN YOU FIND SUCH HEATHEN AS THESE?"

"WE HAVE TRUSTED THE LORD FOR OUR SUPPORT. WE CAN TRUST HIM AGAIN."

1865. JULY 2. EAST LONDON. OFF WHITECHAPEL ROAD. A MEETING WAS ADVERTISED IN A TENT IN A DISUSED QUAKER BURIAL GROUND. 200 TO 300 — SOME STRAIGHT FROM THE PUBS — TURNED UP.

COME AND JOIN US

PRAYER MEETING AT THE QUAKER GROUND

BOOTH UPBRAIDED THEM WITH FIERY ELOQUENCE. "KNEEL AND BE SAVED." SIX CAME FORWARD.

TOO POOR TO PAY FOR TRANSPORT, HE WALKED EIGHT MILES TO HAMMERSMITH, HOME AND WIFE.

"I HAVE FOUND MY DESTINY."

TOGETHER THEY DECIDED TO CONVERT THE WORLD.

1865. SEPTEMBER. A GALE TORE DOWN HIS TENT. BOOTH MOVED HIS MEETINGS TO ANY SHELTER HE COULD FIND. DANCE HALL, THEATRE, WAREHOUSE AND HAYLOFT.

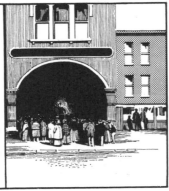

HIRING HALLS COST CASH. HE GATHERED CHILDREN ROUND HIM IN THE STREET. GOT THEM TO SING WITH HIM TILL ADULTS ARRIVED. DRUNKS FROM PUBS. TO LAUGH AND SNEER. SOME STAYED ON TO LISTEN.

A SUNDAY EVENING. BOOTH TOOK BRAMWELL, HIS ELDEST SON, TO A PUB DOOR. GAS JETS LIT HARDENED DRINKERS, DISHEVELLED WOMEN HOLDING INFANTS IN ARMS. BREATHING FUMES OF TOBACCO AND DRINK.

"THESE ARE OUR PEOPLE. THESE ARE THE PEOPLE I WANT YOU TO LIVE FOR AND BRING TO CHRIST."

Published by arrangement with the *Daily Mail*, London.

1868. CHRISTMAS MORNING. BOOTH ROSE EARLY TO PREACH IN WHITECHAPEL. WALKED HOME THROUGH STREETS FULL OF DRUNKS, PAST HOMES WITHOUT FOOD. TO JOIN HIS FAMILY CELEBRATIONS.

HE REACHED HOME PALE AND HAGGARD.

"I'LL NEVER HAVE A CHRISTMAS DAY LIKE THIS AGAIN. THE POOR HAVE NOTHING BUT THE PUBLIC HOUSE."

NEXT CHRISTMAS. CATHERINE COOKED 300 DINNERS. BEEF, PLUM PUDDING AND TEA. BOOTH AND BRAMWELL TOOK THEM TO THE SLUMS.

BY 1872 HE HAD FIVE SHOPS. SELLING HOT SOUP. AND A THREE-COURSE DINNER FOR 6d.

1873. MIDDLESBROUGH, YORKSHIRE. GEORGE RAILTON, 24, METHODIST MINISTER'S SON, READ A REPORT BY BOOTH. LEFT HIS JOB TO VISIT HIM.

WAS ENROLLED AS SECRETARY OF A GROWING MISSION WITH BRANCHES IN SUSSEX AND KENT.

1876. ELIJAH CADMAN, EX-CHIMNEY-SWEEP AND BOXER, HEARD BOOTH SPEAK. ENROLLED AS A MISSION EVANGELIST. WAS POSTED TO WHITBY. PROCLAIMED HIMSELF "CAPTAIN CADMAN OF THE HALLELUJAH ARMY".

1878. A MISSION REPORT CALLED IT A "VOLUNTEER ARMY". BOOTH CROSSED OUT "VOLUNTEER". WROTE IN "SALVATION". THE REV. BOOTH BECAME GENERAL BOOTH. COMMANDER OF THE SALVATION ARMY.

1878. THE ARMY HAD GROWN TO 81 STATIONS. MANNED BY 127 OFFICERS AND 1,900 VOLUNTEERS. SOMETIMES REVILED. MORE OFTEN IGNORED OR UNNOTICED.

SALISBURY. A MARKET PLACE MEETING. CHARLES FRY, BUILDER AND LEADER OF THE LOCAL METHODIST ORCHESTRA, ARRIVED WITH HIS FAMILY. BRINGING THEIR BRASS INSTRUMENTS WITH THEM.

THE SALVATION ARMY BAND WAS BORN.

POPULAR TUNES – "OLD FOLKS AT HOME" AND "HERE'S TO GOOD OLD WHISKY" – WERE GIVEN NEW WORDS. ARMY MEETINGS PROVIDED POPULAR ENTERTAINMENT. TO COMPETE WITH MUSIC HALLS. BOOTH APPROVED.

"WHY SHOULD THE DEVIL HAVE ALL THE BEST TUNES?"

1879. VICTORIAN BRITAIN LOVED UNIFORMS. CADMAN ADDRESSED AN ARMY WAR CONGRESS.

"I WOULD LIKE TO WEAR A SUIT OF CLOTHES THAT WOULD LET EVERYBODY KNOW I MEANT WAR TO THE TEETH AND SALVATION FOR THE WORLD."

CADMAN AND RAILTON DONNED DISTINCTIVE HATS WITH ARMY CRESTS. CAPTAINS WORE BLUE SERGE JACKETS OVER RED JERSEYS. WOMEN MOVED INTO PRINCESS ROBES, PIONEERED BY THE PRINCESS OF WALES.

CATHERINE BOOTH CHOSE A BLACK STRAW HALLELUJAH BONNET. CAPTAIN ANNIE LOCKWOOD, EX-MILLINER, TRIMMED IT WITH A PLEATED BAND OF BLACK SILK ROUND THE CROWN. AND GAVE IT STYLE.

THE LASSES WERE READY FOR BATTLE.

51

1880. FEB. 14. GEORGE RAILTON AND SEVEN ARMY LASSES SAILED FOR NEW YORK. ARMED WITH **ARMY** VERSES TO *"OLD FOLKS AT HOME"* AND *"MY OLD KENTUCKY HOME"*. TO CONQUER **AMERICA.**

MARCH 14. **RAILTON** HELD HIS FIRST MEETING. IN A **NEW YORK** VARIETY THEATRE. NO ONE CAME FORWARD.

HE ESTABLISHED HIS H.Q. IN A **CONVERTED BROTHEL.** *PREACHED TO DRUNKARDS, HARLOTS AND BUMS.*

MAY. HE CABLED **BOOTH.** U.S. FORCES NUMBERED 16 OFFICERS, 40 CADETS, 412 PRIVATES.

EXPEDITIONS WERE SENT TO FRANCE, SWITZERLAND, SWEDEN, CANADA, SOUTH AFRICA, AUSTRALIA, NEW ZEALAND, INDIA AND CEYLON. TO CONQUER THE **WORLD.**

1882. ARMY LASSES FILLED HALLS WITH FERVOUR AND EMPTIED PUBS. DRUNKENNESS DECREASED. SO DID PUBLICANS' PROFITS. BREWERS RETALIATED. *HIRED THUGS TO BREAK UP MEETINGS.*

SHEFFIELD. BOOTH LED A BRASS BAND PROCESSION WITH LIEUT. **EMMERSON DAVISON,** CONVERTED WRESTLER. 1,000 CLOTH-CAPPED **"SHEFFIELD BLADES"** BOMBARDED THEM WITH STONES, AND CHARGED.

DAVISON WAS CARRIED TO HOSPITAL WITH CONCUSSION. SURVIVORS STAGGERED, BATTERED AND BLOODY, TO THEIR HALL. SPECTATORS WERE SHOCKED: **BOOTH** PLEASED — *AT THE PUBLICITY.*

"I LIKE MY RELIGION AS I LIKE MY TEA—HOT."

1882. HASTINGS. SIX SALVATIONISTS BESIEGED. POLICE ARRIVED. THE MOB ATTACKED. CAPTAIN **BEATY** WAS CARRIED WOUNDED TO HIS HOME. HIS WIFE **SUSANNAH** WAS KICKED ALONG THE STREET, LEFT IN A DARK ALLEY UNCONSCIOUS.

917

HER ATTACKER CONFESSED. OFFERED TO SURRENDER TO THE LAW. **SUSANNAH,** IN HOSPITAL, REFUSED.

"TELL HIM I FORGIVE HIM."

SHE DIED. HER MURDERER JOINED THE **SALVATION ARMY.**

IN **ONE YEAR** 56 ARMY BUILDINGS WERE WRECKED: 669 SALVATIONISTS ASSAULTED. JOHN BRIGHT, RADICAL M.P., WROTE TO CATHERINE BOOTH.

"THE PEOPLE WHO MOB YOU WOULD DOUBTLESS HAVE MOBBED THE APOSTLES."

1884. WORTHING. 4,000 THUGS JOINED A "SKELETON ARMY" TO FIGHT SALVATIONISTS. POLICE-SURGEON COLLETT OFFERED £20 FOR *THE FIRST LASSIE THROWN IN THE SEA.* CAPTAIN **ADA SMITH** STOOD FIRM. *"THIS MUST BE FOUGHT OUT."*

SKELETONS BROKE UP MEETINGS. ATTACKED THE SHOP OF GEORGE HEAD, SALVATIONIST, PAINTER AND PLUMBER. HE DREW A PISTOL. OPENED FIRE.

THE MOB FLED. **HEAD** WAS TRIED — AND ACQUITTED.

SHAME-FACED TRADESMEN FORMED VOLUNTEER BODY-GUARDS AT SALVATIONIST MEETINGS. THE **LORD CHIEF JUSTICE,** LORD COLERIDGE, DECLARED SUPPORT.

"WALKING THROUGH THE STREETS, EVEN IF ACCOMPANIED BY MUSIC AND THE SINGING OF HYMNS, IS ABSOLUTELY LAWFUL."

THE **ARMY** BEGAN TO WALK IN PEACE.

1887. QUEEN VICTORIA'S GOLDEN JUBILEE YEAR. *MIDNIGHT ON DECEMBER 1. BOOTH CROSSED **LONDON BRIDGE**. DESTITUTES HUDDLED IN NICHES, SHIVERING UNDER NEWSPAPERS. BLUE WITH COLD.*

NEXT MORNING. **BRAMWELL** CALLED.

"DID YOU KNOW THAT MEN SLEPT OUT ALL NIGHT?"

"WE CAN'T TACKLE EVERY EVIL."

"GO AND DO SOMETHING. GET HOLD OF A WAREHOUSE. HEAT IT. FIND SOMETHING TO COVER THEM."

919

1888. FEB. 18. LIMEHOUSE. THE **ARMY** OPENED A **SHELTER**. HEATED TO **60 DEGREES**. WITH **80** STUFFED LEATHER MATTRESSES AND SHEEPSKIN QUILTS. *FOR ANYONE WITH NOWHERE TO GO.*

1888. MARYLEBONE, LONDON. EVA BOOTH, THE **GENERAL'S** REDHEAD **DAUGHTER**, CLIMBED RICKETY STAIRS TO A GARRET. INSIDE, ON AN IRON BEDSTEAD: AN OLD MAN UNDER A THIN STRIP OF SACKING. *BEDRIDDEN. STARVING. COLD.*

"THANK GOD. IN THE CUPBOARD."

IN THE CUPBOARD SHE FOUND ONE DRY CRUST OF STALE BREAD.

"OH LORD, FOR WHAT I AM ABOUT TO RECEIVE, MAKE ME TRULY THANKFUL."

EVA WEPT AND FLED.

SHE RETURNED WITH FOOD AND KINDLING. TO COOK HIM HIS FIRST HOT MEAL FOR MONTHS. THE **ARMY** DECLARED WAR— ON POVERTY.

1888. VICTORIAN BRITAIN THOUGHT *POVERTY A SIN.* **BOOTH** DISAGREED.

"IT ISN'T WICKED TO BE REDUCED TO RAGS. IT IS NOT A SIN TO STARVE... IT IS SUCH PEOPLE WE MUST HELP."

WEST INDIA DOCK ROAD, LONDON. THE **ARMY** OPENED A **CHEAP FOOD DEPOT.** SELLING *MEAT PUDDING* AND *POTATOES* FOR **3d**: *BAKED JAM ROLL* FOR **½d.**

1890. DESTITUTES STILL NEEDED CASH. THE **ARMY** OPENED BRITAIN'S **FIRST LABOUR EXCHANGE.** PURELY PRIVATE ENTERPRISE. IN **SEVEN YEARS** IT FOUND JOBS FOR **69,000.**

1888. *UNEMPLOYMENT WAS RISING: SOCIAL SECURITY A DREAM.* **THOUSANDS** WERE WITHOUT PAY, FOOD AND HOMES. **BOOTH** LAUNCHED A NEW CRUSADE. *"EVERY CAB HORSE HAS FOOD, SHELTER AND WORK."*

FEB. 15. BRISTOL. CATHERINE ADDRESSED A MEETING.

"GOD WANTS ALL WE ARE, ALL WE ACQUIRE AND ALL WE CAN DO— *TO THE END OF OUR DAYS.*"

SHE HAD JUST DISCOVERED A PAINFUL LUMP ON HER LEFT BREAST.

FEB. 21. **LONDON.** SHE VISITED A SURGEON. DROVE HOME TO TELL **BOOTH** HIS DIAGNOSIS. **CANCER.** BOOTH WAS SHATTERED.

"IT'S CANCER."

"I DON'T UNDERSTAND IT."

1890. A VILLA AT CLACTON. **BOOTH** WATCHED **HIS** WIFE DYING IN PAIN.

"WHY DOES GOD ALLOW THIS? HOW CAN IT BE?"

OCT. 2. **CATHERINE** WEAKENED. THE FAMILY WATCHED. SHE SLID HER WEDDING RING FROM HER FINGER TO HIS.

"BY THIS TOKEN WE WERE UNITED FOR A TIME. BY IT NOW WE ARE UNITED FOR ETERNITY."

OCT. 4. **CATHERINE** DIED. **BOOTH** MADE A NEW VOW.

"MY WORK IS TO FILL UP THE WEEKS, THE DAYS AND THE HOURS. WHEN I HAVE SERVED CHRIST AND MY GENERATION, SHE WILL BID ME WELCOME TO THE SKIES."

1890. OCT. 4. **CATHERINE** DIED. OCT. 20. **BOOTH** PUBLISHED "IN DARKEST ENGLAND". HIS MESSAGE: THREE MILLION, ONE TENTH OF BRITAIN, WERE STARVING, HOMELESS OR DESTITUTE.

IT SOLD **200,000** COPIES IN A **YEAR**. MADE **£7,383** FOR A **DARKEST ENGLAND FUND**. APPEALS AND MEETINGS RAISED **£102,559**.

"WHAT VALUE DO WE PUT ON A HUMAN LIFE AND A HUMAN SOUL?"

IN **LONDON** SEVEN RELIEF STATIONS DISTRIBUTED *LOAVES AND CHEESE*. TEN SHELTERS PROVIDED *BEDS* FROM **1d.** TO **6d.** – **2½P** – A NIGHT. AND A *SUPPER OF BREAD, MEAT AND TEA* FOR **3d.** EACH SHELTER DISPLAYED A NOTICE.

NO MAN NEED BEG, STEAL, STARVE, SLEEP OUT AT NIGHTS, BE A PAUPER OR COMMIT SUICIDE. WE WILL HELP YOU.

1891. HADLEIGH, ESSEX. DOWN-AND-OUTS WERE A FINANCIAL BURDEN. **BOOTH** OPENED AN **ARMY FARM** TO GIVE THEM WORK. CULTIVATING **3,000 ACRES**. *BAKING BRICKS. LEARNING SKILLS* TO START A NEW LIFE IN THE COLONIES.

BOOTH TOOK **CECIL RHODES**, **CAPE COLONY PREMIER** AND **FOUNDER OF RHODESIA**, TO SEE IT. **RHODES** WAS IMPRESSED. TOLD **BRAMWELL**.

"I AM TRYING TO MAKE NEW COUNTRIES. YOUR FATHER IS MAKING NEW MEN."

CHURCHILL BECAME A FRIEND: **LORD NORTHCLIFFE**, FOUNDER OF THE **DAILY MAIL**, A WARM SUPPORTER.

"ALL THE RELIGION I HAVE I OWE TO GENERAL BOOTH."

1904. **BOOTH** WAS SUMMONED TO **BUCKINGHAM PALACE**. FOR AN **AUDIENCE WITH EDWARD VII**. HE WASHED HIS HANDS IN A WORKMAN'S BUCKET. AND SET OFF TO MEET THE **KING**.

"YOU ARE DOING A GREAT WORK, GENERAL BOOTH. HOW DO THE CHURCHES VIEW YOUR WORK NOW?"

"SIR, THEY IMITATE ME."

THE **KING** PRODUCED HIS **AUTOGRAPH ALBUM**. **BOOTH** WROTE.

Some men's ambition is Art.
Some men's ambition is Fame.
Some men's ambition is Gold.
My ambition is the
Souls of men

NEWSPAPERS DROPPED QUOTATION MARKS ROUND HIS TITLE. AND CALLED HIM SIMPLY *THE GENERAL*.

1909. BOOTH WAS 80. THE AUTOMOBILE HAD ARRIVED. HE SET OUT ON HIS SIXTH MOTORCADE. TO COVER 1,460 MILES IN FIVE WEEKS. AND REACH EVERY CORNER OF BRITAIN.

NEWPORT, MONMOUTHSHIRE. HIS EYE WAS TORTURED BY GRIT. A DOCTOR WAS CALLED TO EXAMINE IT.

"DOCTOR, I CAN'T SEE YOU."

"TURN AND LOOK AT THE LIGHT, GENERAL."

"I SEE NO LIGHT. I AM BLIND."

"YES, GENERAL, I AM AFRAID YOU ARE."

"GOD HAS HELPED ME THROUGH MANY A STORM AND HE WILL HELP ME THROUGH THIS."

1912. LONDON. THE ALBERT HALL. BOOTH ADDRESSED HIS LAST MEETING.

"WHILE WOMEN WEEP, AS THEY DO NOW, I'LL FIGHT. WHILE LITTLE CHILDREN GO HUNGRY, I'LL FIGHT. WHILE THERE REMAINS ONE DARK SOUL WITHOUT THE LIGHT OF GOD, I'LL FIGHT TO THE VERY END."

A LAST OPERATION ON HIS LEFT EYE. IT FAILED. HE SENSED BRAMWELL KNEELING BY THE BED.

"I SHALL NEVER SEE YOUR FACE AGAIN. I HAVE DONE WHAT I COULD FOR GOD AND THE PEOPLE WITH MY EYES. NOW I SHALL SEE WHAT I CAN DO WITHOUT MY EYES."

EVA RETURNED FROM AMERICA, DESCRIBED THE GLORY OF THE SUNSET.

"I CANNOT SEE IT, BUT I SHALL SEE THE DAWN."

1912. AUGUST. BOOTH CLOSE TO DEATH.

"BRAMWELL, LOOK AFTER THE HOMELESS."

"YES, GENERAL, I PROMISE."

"IF YOU DON'T, I SHALL COME BACK AND HAUNT YOU."

AUGUST 18. HE LOST CONSCIOUSNESS. AUGUST 20. ALL MOVEMENT STOPPED.

"THIS IS DEATH, DOCTOR?"

"YES, THIS IS DEATH."

"NOW HE IS WITH OUR MOTHER."

BRAMWELL KISSED HIS FOREHEAD FOR THE LAST TIME.

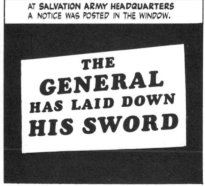

AT SALVATION ARMY HEADQUARTERS A NOTICE WAS POSTED IN THE WINDOW.

THE GENERAL HAS LAID DOWN HIS SWORD

AUGUST 28. LONDON. 34,000 FILLED OLYMPIA TO SEE THE GENERAL LIE IN STATE. AMONG THEM, UNRECOGNISED, QUEEN MARY. CLOSE TO A PROSTITUTE.

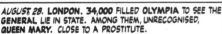

Where will YOU spend

"HE CARED FOR THE LIKES OF US."

AUGUST 29. 10,000 UNIFORMED SALVATIONISTS MARCHED THROUGH LONDON BEHIND THE COFFIN. TO A NEW SONG WITH AN OLD TUNE.

"THERE'S NO FRIEND LIKE JESUS, THERE'S NO PLACE LIKE HOME."

OFFICES WERE SHUTTERED: CROWDS IN TEARS. SALVATIONISTS HELD THEIR HEADS HIGH. THE GENERAL WAS NOT DEAD. HE WAS PROMOTED TO GLORY. HE HAD LEFT BEHIND HIS ARMY TO FIGHT ON FOR GOD

"WELL DONE, THOU GOOD AND FAITHFUL SERVANT."

THE END.

Good Ca

A Song for Guides
by Sheila Deft

1. Our Patrol went to camp on a fine weekend in spring.
  We took all of our equipment and our food and everything.
  We had meat and we had vegetables and lots of seasoning,
  For we planned to make a good camp stew.

Chorus: In a good camp stewpan we planned to make a good camp stew.

2. The first thing we did when we reached our camping-site
  Was to pitch the tents and get unpacked and get the fire alight.
  We forgot to bring a spoon but found a tentpeg worked all right
  For stirring up the good camp stew.

Chorus: In a good camp stewpan, for stirring up the good camp stew.

3. To make some camping gadgets was essential, we were told,
  And the thought of eating off the floor made all our blood run cold;
  But the table-legs kept falling down — the lashing wouldn't hold,
  So we stuck them on with good camp stew.

Chorus: From the good camp stewpan, we stuck them on with good camp stew.

4. Well, the rain came down, and the place was like a flood.
  There was just a little island where the fireplace had stood.
  You have heard of coffee-grounds before — well, now there's gravy mud!
  And you stir it into good camp stew.

Chorus: In a good camp stewpan, you stir it into good camp stew.

5. With our aids to navigation we went climbing on the fell.
  We had compasses and maps and whistles — lamps we had as well.
  But for coming home we simply navigated by the smell,
  For we recognised a good camp stew.

Chorus: In a good camp stewpan, we recognised a good camp stew.

p Stew

Tune: **The Golden Vanity**
or **John Brown's Body**

6. To keep the country tidy is our duty to the Queen,
   And we picked up lots of litter where some litter-louts had been,
   But we had to put it somewhere, so to keep the campsite clean
   We tipped it in the good camp stew.

Chorus: In the good camp stewpan, we tipped it in the good camp stew.

7. Now visits from Commissioners are something we deplore,
   But we have to make them welcome, 'cos they're folk we can't ignore.
   Still, they never seem to hang around at mealtimes any more
   Since we fed them on our good camp stew.

Chorus: From the good camp stewpan, we fed them all on good camp stew.

8. Now mothers are inclined to fuss — I guess they always will,
   But our Guiders wouldn't let us camp without some camping skill,
   And we know exactly what to do if anyone is ill —
   We cure everything with good camp stew.

Chorus: From a good camp stewpan, we cure everything with good camp stew.

9. Our training programme paves the way for happy, useful lives
   As parents in tomorrow's world, and when that day arrives
   There'll be lots of splendid men and lots of most accomplished wives,
   Raising families on good camp stew.

Chorus: From a good camp stewpan, there is nothing like a good camp stew.

STEW PAN

FINDING FIREMARKS

by P. Thompson

The Sun Company firemark

One of the suggestions in the *Guide Handbook* is that you gain "Fun From Buildings," so look for firemarks.

Whole streets of houses and shops went up in flames around the time of the Great Fire of London. Many towns had to be completely rebuilt after such disasters. Among them were Warwick, Northampton, Dorchester and Stratford-on-Avon.

If your property was destroyed by fire there was no fire-insurance to help you. You were dependent on the assistance of members of your Guild, or else you were given licence to beg!

However, when stone rather than wood began to be used more in building, the fire risk became less and in the late seventeenth century fire-insurance companies began to be set up. Each company had to organise its own fire-brigade with a distinctive uniform; public fire-fighting equipment was very primitive, even where it was available.

These brigades could only attend fires at the property of people insured with their particular company. So, in order to identify the houses insured, "firemarks" were issued; these were affixed to the outside of buildings at first-floor height or above.

The firemarks had to withstand the weather, so were usually made of lead, or, later, of copper or iron. Each had the trademark of the insurance company stamped on it, and beneath this was the number of the policy of the owner

The Alliance Company firemark

date as costs went up, for they were cheaper to make and really acted as advertisements for the companies concerned.

Make a note of where you find the marks; they will be useful if your Patrol decides to try for the Explorer Pennant.

It is good to know that nowadays an efficiently trained fire crew will be quickly on the scene of a fire, without having to stop and peer about for firemarks. Certainly they will not have to contend with a rival brigade. That of another fire-insurance company would sometimes hinder those trying to put out the blaze and hoping to prove their inefficiency to bystanders and thus gain more business for their own company.

of the property. A gilded face of the sun on a blue background obviously belonged to the Sun Company, and this mark is widely found. Others included Atlas, the god carrying the world on his shoulders; Phoenix, with the legendary bird, rather like an eagle, rising from its own ashes; and a castle. The Royal Exchange Assurance had a representation of the old Royal Exchange building in London. Others simply had the name of the company above the policy number.

There is a splendid collection of firemarks in the Castle Museum at York, and some examples in most county museums. But it is more fun to try to track down the marks where they still exist on some older buildings. They are often discoloured with age; occasionally they are painted over, but you can usually decipher the trademark if you look carefully.

Those which have no number beneath are called "fire plates." These were introduced at a later

The London Company firemark

Do-it-Yourself Fancy Dress

DELPHINE EVANS Suggests Gags, Ideas, Characters and Do-It-Yourself Costumes for Your Company Show or Fancy-Dress Party

It's fun and economical to make your own fancy dress, costumes, etc. for party or stage show. Here are some suggestions. **Old Clothes, Shoes, Etc.** Anything old will help to turn yourselves into tramps or gipsies. With an old pram or cart filled with junk you could perform a sketch as Steptoe & Son or as Dustbin Men.

Crepe-Paper Birds. Crepe paper is excellent for turning yourselves into birds, butterflies or flowers.

For birds or butterflies cut crepe paper into the shape of wings, making one side the length of an arm. Attach this to your outstretched arms and make either a helmet with feelers for a butterfly or a helmet with a cardboard beak attached for a bird. Tights and jumpers in colour or crepe wound round will make a butterfly or bird "body".

For flowers, cut large petal shapes out of crepe paper, attach to a wire frame and place around the face. Body and arms should be green to represent stem and leaves. Sunflowers, pansies and tulips are some of the flowers that can be represented.

By using green on its own, you can make yourself into a Christmas tree. Decorate it with tinsel and small parcels.

Silver Foil is ideal for making a Jack Frost covered in icicles. It can also make a spaceman or a Martian, to which you can add extra arms, eyes and feelers.

Witches and Wizards. A cloak draped round the shoulders and a long pointed hat can quickly produce a witch or a wizard.

Red Riding Hood. Turn yourself or a Brownie sister into Red Riding Hood with a red raincoat complete with hood. With a

"Period" costumes can be made to look very effective

Guides and Scouts in a scene from "Cinderella"

basket of goodies to carry, the character is complete and unmistakable.

Nursery-Rhyme Characters. Bridesmaids' dresses are ideal for many nursery-rhyme characters, and "props" could include a bowl and an imitation spider for Little Miss Muffet, a watering-can and flowers for Mary, Mary, Quite Contrary, a shepherd's crook and a toy lamb for Little Bo-Peep, and a cardboard crown, a cut-out of playing-card "hearts" and a tray of tarts for the Queen of Hearts.

Small boys or girls could be turned into Little Boy Blue (dressed all in blue), Wee Willie Winkie (in pyjamas, with torch), and Little Jack Horner (with thumb in pie). Two Guides suitably dressed could be Jack and Jill or Jack Spratt and his wife, one fat and one thin.

Historical Characters. Costumes for these may be more expensive and more difficult to make, but they offer scope for interesting portrayals or sketches. Henry VIII and any of his wives, Napoleon, Nelson, Joan of Arc, and Florence Nightingale are a few of the many characters of history that will be easily recognisable at

a fancy-dress party or on the stage. Look through an illustrated history-book for details of costumes of the period. You will need skill—and perhaps Mum's help—in making suitable costumes, but the result will probably be quite striking.

National Costumes. It's fairly easy to find pictures of a Dutch boy or girl, a Hawaiian maiden, Chinese girls, or cowboys and Indians. It might be best to portray a national whose dress is not too difficult to make.

Sporting Personalities. Well-known tennis stars and other sportswomen in the news make good central characters for sketches. Shorts and shirts and similar garments can easily be adapted to portray them.

TV Characters. These are always a hit with audiences, and they can include characters known to young children watching—such as the Flintstones, the Diddymen, the Wombles, or any others in current programmes. Pop stars can be imitated by Guides with a flair for this kind of entertainment, and can be the cue for a song.

Humorous Gags. Here are some

"gags" that are guaranteed to get a laugh: "A Clean Sweep", a chimney-sweeper dressed completely in white. "The M.P. Who Lost His Seat", a character with bowler hat, striped trousers and rolled umbrella, but minus the seat of his trousers. "Chip Off the Old Block", a figure covered in wood shavings. "No More Strikes", with used matches sewn all over the figure. "Melancholy Baby", a Guide dressed as a baby and carrying a melon and a cauliflower. "Sunshine Girl", a Guide dressed all in yellow. "In the Pink", a character dressed all in pink. "Feeling Blue", a Guide dressed all in blue and looking downcast. "Plain and Purl", a plain Guide (or Scout) and a pretty Guide.

Box "Props". Among stage properties that can easily be made are a "Jack-in-the-Box", a grandfather-clock case, and a telephone kiosk.

Half the fun of putting on a stage show or going to a fancy-dress party is preparing for it. Let's hope that these ideas will stimulate you into thinking of others and help to make your own participation a great success.

A Slipper Pincushion

Andrew Liston shows you how to make it

A charming pincushion in the shape of a red-and-gold slipper is easy to make and will sell easily on the Guide stall.

Fig. 1. Draw a slipper shape on a piece of card measuring about 15cm (6″) × 5cm (2″), then cut it out.

Fig. 2. Cut a 7.5cm-long (3″) piece of foam plastic to the shape of the heel of the slipper. Cut the front edge of the foam at an angle so that it slopes down towards the card, then glue the plastic in place.

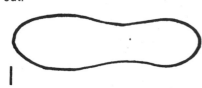

Fig. 3. Place the slipper on a piece of red felt and draw round it. Cut out a felt shape which is 2.5cm (1″) larger all round than the outline of the slipper. Lay the felt shape over the slipper, gluing the edges to the underside.

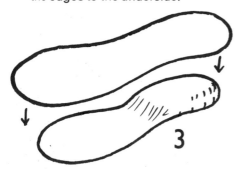

Fig. 4. Tack the edges together on the underside to hold the felt firmly in place.

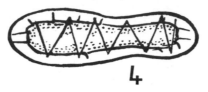

Fig. 5. Cut a red felt toecap shape which is 1.3cm (½″) wider than the slipper at the broadest part of the toecap. Embroider a trefoil or flower design on the toecap with gold coloured embroidery cotton.

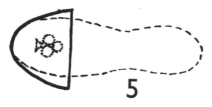

Fig. 6. Sew the toecap to the slipper. Start at the point of the toe and sew towards the heel on each side.

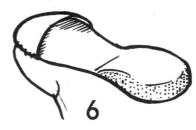

Fig. 7. Cut a piece of red felt, the same size and shape as the slipper, and use adhesive to fix it to the underside. Sew the edges in place all round.

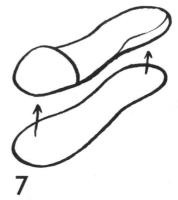

Fig. 8. Starting at the heel, sew a red or gold silk cord all round the slipper, hiding the joints between the sections of felt. Use a short piece of the same cord to sew on a loop at the heel for hanging the slipper.

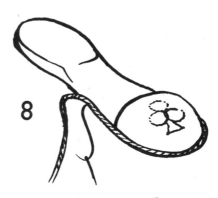

Fig. 9. Tuck a thimble into the toecap, and a selection of pins into the cushioned heel, and your pincushion is complete.

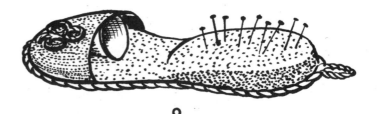

Foxlease, the Girl Guides Association's training centre in the New Forest. The false wall and five blocked windows can be seen in the photograph on the top floor

False Fronts and Blocked Windows

by P. Thompson

If you visit Foxlease, the Guide training house in the New Forest, look hard at the upstairs windows at the front of the building. You will see that they have no glass in them, which seems rather odd.

Foxlease, once "Cox Leyes", was built about four hundred years ago as a house for one of the King's forest-keepers. There are still some parts of the old house left, including the hall and two little rooms at the top, but in 1775 a Georgian building was put around what was left of the original bits. Someone must have thought that the jumble of roofs and different styles of architecture was rather untidy, so a false

front was added with mock windows in it. You can see the back of this false wall from the window of one of the Quiet Rooms at the top of the house.

Other large houses adopted this idea too, so look out for them.

More commonly seen are windows that have been bricked up. For one hundred and fifty years there was a tax payable by householders that depended on the number of windows in their house—the more windows, the higher the tax! If you had ten or more windows the amount to be paid increased. Therefore many of the blocked-up windows that

you see were bricked in by people trying to cut down their taxes, although some may be due to the alteration of rooms by a new owner. There was a great deal of agitation to repeal this law, and it eventually ended in 1851. So the majority of houses with blocked-up windows were built before this date.

Now we can have as many windows as we want in our homes, although as rates are affected by the number of rooms in a house things are not that much different!

Guides in "Tom Thumb" Town

Written and photographed by V. Hinton

We were a small party of Guides—four Patrol Leaders, two Seconds, Lefty and me, the Guider—and we were on holiday in Holland. We rented a house in Rotterdam and did our own shopping and cooking—and great fun it was!

One day we set off early to spend the day in The Hague, which is the city in which the Dutch Parliament meets. We were told that we must not miss seeing Madurodam, which is Holland's "Tom Thumb" town.

Outside the Central Station at The Hague we boarded a No. 9 tram. This took us through the centre of the town. In fifteen minutes we were at the gates of Madurodam, which is claimed to be the largest model village in the world, though it is more like a town than a village.

Once inside the gates, we followed arrows painted on the paths and wound our way past old and new Dutch buildings reproduced in exact detail about eighty times smaller than their originals. Everything is in miniature, including trees, model animals and people. There are tiny replicas of very old buildings, including the Hall of the Knights, the meeting-place of Parliament, in The Hague. There are old churches and a Town Hall with a wedding taking place in it. Dutch weddings must always be carried out at the Town Hall. If a church ceremony is desired, this must take place after the ceremony in the Town Hall.

There are modern buildings too—Government offices, a civic centre, and a big secondary school. In one corner there is a village fair. We put a one-cent piece in a box, and everything at the fair began to work and music to play. We were all fascinated.

Farther along the paths, we came to a recreation ground with a football stadium, a swimming-pool, cycling and racing tracks, and a boating pool—all of Tom Thumb size.

A little way on we reached the docks, with ships moving round the tiny harbour and others being loaded and unloaded. One boat caught fire at intervals, very realistically, and a fire-fighting tender came along and put the fire out with jets of water.

Near the docks is an aerodrome, with planes taxi-ing along the runway, and others stationary, with people getting in and out of them. The planes bear the markings of many different countries.

Going round across the town is a model railway with a big central station and several smaller ones. As we walked round, these little model trains ran past; there is a fast transcontinental train, a goods train, and smaller passenger trains; they go over bridges, through cuttings and along embankments all beautifully landscaped with miniature plants.

There is also a motorway with every conceivable kind of motor transport on it. There is even a car crash with police-car, ambulance and attendants on the scene. As this is Holland, there are inevitably canals with locks and windmills. The last scene we passed was one of Dutch bulb-fields with rows and rows of tiny flowers—a fascinating sight.

So interesting and unusual is this "Tom Thumb" town that the Guides wanted to go round again —and there was no dissenting voice!

Stooping down, the Guides could still look down on the rooftops

A Dutch canal on a tiny scale

A square one-eightieth the size of the real one

The Hall of the Knights

The Town Hall

A—E

SO YOU'VE WON A BADGE!

Crisp Comments by Daphne M. Pilcher

Arts and Crafts Emblem

So you've won a badge! Congratulations! Your Guider has presented it, and someone—do I dare say you?—has sewn it on. Ah, but what use are you going to make of it? Winning it is not the end of it. It is only the gateway, the very beginning.

In your Promise you undertook to make good use of your time. A badge stitched to your sleeve and forgotten is a waste of your time and the time of your tester. If it is a badge towards your Arts and Crafts emblem, it would be a waste to learn a skill and then not use it.

How can you make use of these skills? First, pass them on! Other members of your Patrol may very well be interested in finding out how something is done. Be truthful, did you really learn something new, or did you take the test because it was something you knew already? Well, whatever the answer, you can still put that badge to use.

If your Patrol or your Company should need to fill a stall at a church garden-party or bazaar or other money-raising effort, put the Guide Motto into practice, BE PREPARED.

Knotter badge—How about making string bags? They are always useful. Just remember to keep an eye on the size of your hole. Don't forget coloured string. A combination of colours makes a gay result.

Basket Maker badge—Raffia mats are always acceptable. Each member of the Patrol could make

Carpenter Badge

Basket Maker Badge

Artist Badge

Knotter Badge

Toymaker Badge

66

one of a different colour and they could be used singly or as a set. Perhaps you are rather more ambitious. Try making waste-paper baskets.

Stitchery badge—What about small embroidered pictures? If a design presents difficulties for you, look round the Company for an Artist badge and go into partnership with its owner. Find a Guide with the Carpenter badge and frame your picture.

Knitter badge—Knit a soft toy. This might start you on the Toymaker badge. The first clause of the Toymaker test requires you to *make a toy of your own choice*. Are there several Arts and Crafts emblems among your Guides? Exchange skills and all try for the Arts and Crafts emblem.

So take a good look at those badges and get down to work. Earn the right to keep wearing them!

If you haven't any badges yet, make a start—now!

Stitchery Badge

Knitter Badge

"Of course there's an underfelt — it's grass!"

GUIDERS, SELL YOUR SKILLS!

Contributions for the *Girl Guide Annual* and the *Brownie Annual* are welcomed throughout the year. Short, complete stories, articles, puzzles, how-to-makes, verse, etc., related to Guiding are required and paid for soon after acceptance; so are black-and-white photographs and colour slides and prints of Guiding activities. Please put name and address on all pictures and enclose a brief factual description of each subject. Colour will be returned after use. Send, enclosing stamped and fully addressed envelope, to THE EDITOR, GUIDING ANNUALS, PURNELL BOOKS, BERKSHIRE HOUSE, QUEEN STREET, MAIDENHEAD, SL6 1NF.

Flower and Plant Quiz

Set and illustrated
by Michael P. Edwards

1. This plant can be seen on the banks of streams in March. What is it?

2. These sulphur-coloured flowers are common on waste ground in spring. What are they?

3. The yellow flowers of this tree are often called pussy willow. What is the proper name of the tree?

4. This odd-looking plant appears in the hedge-rows in spring. What is its name?

5. This plant is common during the summer months. What is it?

CAMPING DAYS

The 26th Leicester Guide Company in camp on a beautiful lakeside site at Ampleforth, Yorkshire

Colour slides by Mrs J. Wetzig

MAKE MAPS THAT MEAN SOMETHING

by R. Brook

MAP READER BADGE

The Guide Map Reader badge develops skill in *using* maps, understanding conventional symbols, interpreting grid references, and the like. But don't overlook the fascination of actually *making* maps of your own.

Guides interested in natural history may have read such books by Gerald Durrell as *The New Noah, The Overloaded Ark,* and *My Family and Other Animals.* In the latter he writes about the ''picture maps'', which a tutor encouraged him to make as a boy. He says, *Our maps were works*

of art. The principal volcanoes belched such flames and sparks one feared they would set the paper continents alight; the mountain ranges of the world were so blue and white with ice and snow that it made one chilly to look at them. Our oceans . . . were full of life . . . bland and innocent-looking octopi tenderly engulfed small boats in their arms; Chinese junks with jaundiced crews were followed by shoals of well-dentured sharks, while fur-clad Eskimoes pursued herds of walrus through icefields thickly populated by bears and

penguins. *They were maps that lived . . . maps that really meant something!*

Well, that's the idea! It needn't be China seas and Arctic icefloes. It can be your own neighbourhood, your summer camp-site, your last weekend hike.

The first step is to make a rough pencil map of the area you propose to deal with, marking on it all the possible items of interest you can discover. Never mind at this stage about having too much material. You can always be selective later, leaving out less important material or that which does not lend itself easily to illustration.

Obvious things to mark are buildings of various kinds—churches, castles, bridges, market-crosses, stately homes, If you can make rough sketches or collect pictures of these it will help considerably when you come to make the map itself.

Then there are natural features that will lend themselves to colourful illustration—rivers, copses, lakes, hills, rocks. Notice what kinds of trees the woods are composed of. You may be able to represent these fairly accurately on your map.

Next look for man-made features (other than the buildings already mentioned). Mines, quarries and mills all provide illustrative material. The products

of the factories may, too—shoes, cars, chocolates, pottery, cutlery, cheese, bread. It all depends on where you live, of course, but if you are in a town there may be a variety of products you can include.

Don't forget local history. Is the birthplace of some celebrity near by? Did a famous traveller of the past—John Wesley, William Cobbett, Daniel Defoe, George Fox—visit the district? If so, this certainly deserves mention and, if possible, a portrait!'

Thinking in terms of history, most towns have a coat-of-arms. This can decorate your map suitably at some point. Now you have material sufficient and more than sufficient to get you going.

For the groundwork of your map you will need a large sheet of cartridge paper, or, better still, thin cardboard. First, sketch lightly in pencil the main features of the area—rivers, roads, hills, lakes, woods (or, if you are doing

N
E
W
S

RUINS
FOREST

COUNTY ARMS

LAKE

QUARRY

MILL

CLAPPER
BRIDGE

WOOLLEN
CLOTH

DOLMAN

PATH

STILE

PATH

NATURE RESERVE

CURRENT

QUAY

VIKINGS

SAILING

LOC

THE DUKE

STATELY HOME

DEER PARK

BUS STOP

TOWN

FARM

CAVES

SMUGGLERS INN

GUIDE CAMP

TEA CLIPPERS

LIGHTHOUSE

a town or village area, streets and principal buildings).

When you are satisfied with the accuracy of what you have done in this respect, sketch in your pictorial features — buildings, characters, local products, etc. It is better to do this before boldly marking in roads, rivers, etc., because the pictures may to some extent overlap the other features, and you can best allow for this by doing *both* in pencil first, then erasing lines you do not need in your final product. Moreover, if you are not careful at the first attempt, the tendency is to make the pictures rather too large for the map.

To correct this, remember that you will not have room for a great deal of *detail* in your drawings. It is the *general effect* you must aim at, the *impression* of a castle or stately home rather than a photographic type of reproduction.

Only when this preliminary planning is complete should you proceed to bold outline and colouring. Felt-tip pens of various thicknesses are probably the most suitable instruments, though for lettering you may find a mapping-pen useful. Again, it is useful to pencil in names first and then *check* your spelling and copying carefully. It is all too easy to miss out a letter or make some similar error, and so spoil the whole effect.

Finally, if you want to be really ambitious and outdo even Gerald Durrell's "maps that meant something", you can, instead of "flat" pictures on the map, make your illustrations "cut-out" ones. This can be done by cutting round all but the base of the drawing, and then pushing it upwards so that it stands upright.

It is probably more satisfactory, however, if you want a relief-map, to draw the buildings, woods, hills, historical figures, etc, on separate pieces of thin card with a tab at the bottom snipped in the centre with a pair of scissors, so that half folds forward and half backwards. This can then be glued to the base of the map, with quite realistic effect.

ADVENTURE

by Mary E. Ramsay

Have you enjoyed camping with the Guide Company? Do you long to take to the hills, or pack a canoe with your gear and spend a few days with friends canoeing along a quiet river . . . and then camping overnight or using a nearby Youth Hostel?

These are the kind of activities that are at their best in the Ranger group—and many Ranger Units have far more opportunity to take part in a wide range of adventurous pursuits than is possible in the Guide Company, mainly because much of the programme can be built round these activities.

Photo by Mike Meredith

Learning to climb during a Ranger course at Whernside Manor, the caving and mountaineering centre among the Yorkshire Dales

WITH RANGERS

Julie and Johanna Goodson and Christine Burridge sail from Denmark to Germany on a pre-investiture Ranger challenge

For instance, the 1st Anytown Rangers are planning to go rock-climbing in the summer, and are already making preparations for this. They have made contact with their local Scout/Guide Mountaineering Club for expert help and instruction from an instructor with a Mountain Leadership Certificate, and are already making or gathering together some of the equipment they will need. The programme includes valley walks and rambles, practising map-reading, and building up their walking ability. Good walking-boots are essential for long distances, but the Rangers are making their own waterproof clothing (cagoules and over-trousers) and back-packs.

When they are more experienced, they plan to progress to mountain walks and scrambles, and then to get basic training on easy climbs such as at Bowles Rocks, in Kent, or other practice slopes. When they have the funds, the climax of their training will be a visit to Glenbrook, the Girl Guides Association's Outdoor Activities Training Centre near Sheffield, or another mountaineering centre where there are qualified instructors and all the equipment necessary is available.

The 2nd Freetown Rangers are more interested in exploring lowland country. They are studying orienteering as a sport and as a means of exploring areas of the British Isles they have not visited before—such as the South Downs Way, Dartmoor, Exmoor, the Mendips or the Quantocks or even parts of the Pennine Way if weather conditions are suitable. They will stay in Youth Hostels or other indoor accommodation so that they do not have to carry too much kit, and can then plan their itinerary to include their other interests—brass-rubbing and bird-watching—at the same time.

Other Units, such as the 3rd Hometown Rangers, spend a lot of their time on the water, and are busy during the winter months making fibre-glass canoes from a mould borrowed from the local education authority. Their last canoe was launched in the middle of a thunderstorm, complete with umbrellas for the "crew", but proved its worth and made it possible for some of the Rangers to gain their canoe permits, with the help of an expert from a local club. They plan to gain more canoe permits in the coming months, and then to have a "canoe-camping expedition" when they have made (or managed to borrow) enough canoes to get all the Rangers afloat at the same time. Future plans include instruction in

Rangers follow a route by map and compass

Rangers practise canoe-rolling

dinghy-sailing, if possible on the Norfolk Broads.

Many Ranger units engage in these adventurous activities, and some too include ski-ing, horse-riding, caving, water-ski-ing, gliding, sailing, rowing and swimming as part of their yearly programme. These activities of course depend on the area lived in, and what facilities are available, but if Rangers are really keen the expert instructor (vital for most of these pursuits) is usually available.

Cost prevents some Units from doing as many of these things as they would like, but careful planning in the overall programme (making or borrowing essential equipment), and planned fund-raising, usually enable each Unit to carry out its aim.

Similarly, if you do not want to follow one of these hardy outdoor pursuits the Unit you join may go in for something gentler but perhaps just as adventurous—angling, sketching, following nature-trails, lightweight camping, archery, or rifle-shooting.

The programme is one that allows each Ranger to experiment in whatever subject she wishes, and usually there is a qualification (boating, bathing, camping) that can be aimed for, or an Interest Certificate that can be gained (such as Archery, Climber, Explorer, Gliding, Hill-Walker, Skier, Skin Diver).

So, if you enjoy the out-of-doors and want to try something adventurous, join your local Ranger Unit, and make your dreams a reality. They will welcome you. The possibilities for adventure with Rangers are endless and the things you have done with your Company and Patrol will have prepared you for life in a Ranger Unit.

A tree across a stream and rope handholds give scope for fun to these Malmesbury District Rangers

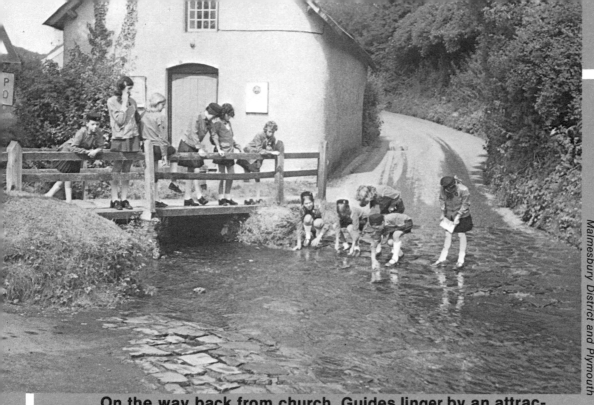

Colour slide by Miss Gillian Bobbett of Guides from Malmesbury District and Plymouth

On the way back from church, Guides linger by an attractive Somerset ford

Summer Days

Hurrah for a dip

Colour slide by Mrs. M. Booth of Guides of the 1st Bishopston Company, Swansea, in camp

FACTS ABOUT FUNGI

Written and photographed by Michael P. Edwards

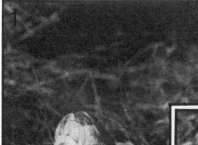

**(1) Shaggy Ink-Cap—
one day old**

**(2) Shaggy Ink-Cap—
a few days old**

**(3) Rough-Stemmed
Boletus**

Mention fungi to most city people and they think of horrid, slimy, umbrella-shaped plants that should be trodden underfoot as soon as their heads push through the earth.

But mycology, as the study of fungi is termed, can be an absorbing pastime. For Guides it can help with the Collector badge and the Naturalist badge.

The best time for a fungus foray is September. Choose fine weather, two or three days after rain. Fungi of all descriptions will be dotted about where a few days earlier there will have been none.

Of the hundreds of species in Britain, only about twelve are deadly poisonous. It's a good idea to become familiar with these by reading books about fungi or by first-hand study with a knowledgeable companion.

Here are some of the common species you are most likely to find:—

Shaggy Ink-Cap, especially on recently cultivated ground. It is often a nuisance on bowling-greens and tennis-courts. The white, barrel-shaped head is 5″ tall and covered with ragged scales—buffish on the crown. When young, this species is edible. After opening like a bell, the Shaggy Ink-Cap begins to blacken from the bottom; this is called liquifying; in the process the spores are suspended in the inky substance, which can be used for writing.

Rough-Stemmed Boletus: You will find this fungus beneath birch-trees during August and September. The brown or greyish cap is 3″ to 4″ across; it is smooth and somewhat moist.

Common Earth-Ball: The bun-shaped fruit-like bodies of this

Collybia Maculata: Like many species of fungi, this does not have a common name. It grows in abundant clumps in woods, especially where there is bracken, under which it prefers to grow. The white cap, 3″ to 5″ across, is spotted with rust-brown in the later stages of growth and is borne on a stem some 5″ tall.

Honey Fungus: This fungus is heartily disliked by the forester, for it attacks the roots of trees and eventually kills them. It may be

(4) Common Earth-Ball

(5) Polyporus

(6) Collybia Maculata

(7) Honey Fungus

fungus are abundant among leaf-litter throughout the autumn. Colour is ochre, but this becomes darker due to weathering. It seems to like bare ground.

Polyporus: There are several kinds of this fungus, which goes under the general name of "bracket fungi". It often grows in tiers on dying birch-tree trunks, where the smooth grey fruit-like bodies are often hoof-shaped. Unlike most fungi, the polyporus is tough and corky. The dried body is 3″ to 6″ across and was once used for stropping razors.

found in large groups at the base of affected stumps and trees. The cap is yellowish-tawny to deep-brown and measure between 2″ and 6″ across.

This fungus is very common on ▶ dying tree-trunks. Its name, *pollystictus versicolour*, comes from its caps of varied colours, which are usually arranged in tiers

▲ Razor-strop fungus (*polyporus betulinus*)

▲ These are orange elf-cups, which can be found in the autumn

This grows at the base of broad-leaved trees in September. Its ◀ name is *pholiota squarrosa*

Strange Incident

A True Story by R. Dellenty

Many years ago I was a Guider in Singapore. There were many nationalities among the Guides and Brownies, and among the Scouts and Cubs too. Most of the boys and girls were very poor.

As Christmas approached, it was decided it would be nice to give presents to underprivileged children. Not only Guides and Brownies but Scouts and Cubs were to ask their parents to let them earn fifty cents each and with the money to buy a present of their own choosing.

A week before Christmas we borrowed a local missionary chapel. The priest in charge, a young Anglican, let us arrange and conduct our own carol service. That evening we all packed into the chapel and began our service. Halfway through, we broke from traditional carols, and the boys and girls were asked to sing "All Things Bright and Beautiful", during which they would bring their presents to the altar.

The first Brownie to come forward carried a large, unclothed baby doll. As the padre laid the doll gently on the altar, it remind-ed us of the real meaning of Christmas. There followed a total of over 380 toys, a really wonderful offering.

During the next few days we sorted toys into bags for boys and girls and as far as possible into age-groups. Off they went to orphanages, hospitals and the leprosy home. Finally, on Christ-mas Eve, we were left with one bag for boys and one bag for girls, with 37 toys in each. Try as we would, we failed to find any home for them. In despair, I asked Quek, a Chinese taxi-driver whose cab I sometimes used, whether he knew of anywhere where the toys would be acceptable. He went off to talk to his friends and came back to me, saying, "Come with me!"

We took the toys and went off in his taxi on a journey that took us some miles. We came to a small track in the Kampong area. I was surprised to hear the sound of singing by children's voices. Suddenly into view came a few small huts, and I read a notice on a board that showed it to be a hospital for spastic children.

A nun came out to the taxi, and I asked her if she would like some toys for the children. She replied that they were having a Christmas party, but had no toys.

I gave her the two bags and explained that there were toys for 37 boys and 37 girls.

As the taxi turned to drive away, the nun called out to us in Chinese. Quek chatted away for a moment, then looked at me and said, "She ask me how you knew they have 37 boys and 37 girls."

The Pony Patrol

Guides of the 1st Chatteris Company, Cambridgeshire, clean up their town and raise £100 in the process for the parish-church
Photo: Mrs G. M. Barrett

◄ **Guides of the 26th Leicester Company demonstrate their acrobatic skill**

Another 26th Leicester Guide tries *her* skill in the camp kitchen
Photos: Mrs J. Wetzig
▼

Guiding

in Pictures

A rope-bridge proves a popular attraction to Gloucestershire Guides at the County Head-quarters "Open Day", Cowley Deer Park

Photo: Robert Moss

◄ Kent Guides make notes of their observations during a nature hike

The 1st Failand Company ▶ Guides made this beau-tiful well-dressing for the local flower festival

Photo: Mrs J. Williams

89

Camping Days Are Here Again

by Jean Howard

Get out of the lorry
And stand in the rain,
Put your kit in the trek-cart
And run down the lane!
Who minds the wet weather?
It's camp time again!

Now pitch the tents quickly
And gather dry wood.
Here's some punk and the matches;
Dead holly is good.
The fire burns up brightly,
We'll soon have hot food.

We sit in a horseshoe
And all join in grace.
The stew is delicious—
It's sunk without trace!
We wash up the dishes,
Put each in its place.

The daylight is fading;
We sing round the fire
New songs and old favourites
Our hearts to inspire.
Then goodnights are said
And to bed we retire.

Answers to Puzzles and Quizzes

HOW'S YOUR ENGLISH GEOGRAPHY? *(p. 33)*

1—Nuneaton, 2—Newquay, 3—Deal, 4—Redruth, 5—Lancaster, 6—Darlington, 7—Sandwich, 8—Eton, 9—Crewe, 10—Barking

GUESS THE WILDFLOWER *(p. 42)*

1—primrose, 2—cowslip, 3—harebell, 4—foxglove, 5—buttercup, 6—sorrel, 7—broom, 8—iris, 9—violet, 10—stitchwort, 11—thrift, 12—ragged robin, 13—thistle, 14—forget-me-not, 15—water crowfoot

FLOWER AND PLANT QUIZ *(p. 68)*

1—butterbur, 2—coltsfoot, 3—goat willow, 4—cuckoo-pint or wild arum, 5—red campion

THE KINGFISHERS' HIKE *(p. 93)*

Bridge, windmill, antiquities, church, spire, main, wood, lake, marsh, main, Youth Hostel, level crossing, unfenced road, station, railway, tunnel, lock, river, bridge, orchard, gravel pit, village, unfenced road, church, tower, post office, bus station

WEIGHTY WORDS *(p. 42)*

1—tonnage, 2—Eton, 3—tone, 4—tongue, 5—tongs, 6—tonic, 7—cretonne, 8—stone, 9—Beeton, 10—stonecrop, 11—Milton, 12—Stilton, 13—Blyton, 14—Hampton Court, 15—stonechat, 16—Clifton, 17—atone, 18—Stonehenge, 19—intone

GRAND £100 PRIZE COMPETITION

Share the Prize Between Yourself and Your Company!

Nothing could be easier than choosing which story, article, puzzle, etc. you like best in this *Girl Guide Annual*, could it?

Well, that's practically all you have to do to stand a chance of winning £50 for your Company and a handsome new bicycle or something else of equal value for yourself.

Simply pick out which you think is the best and next-best story, article, puzzle, etc. from each of the six groups listed below and fill in the entry form accordingly.

The competitor whose choices are nearest those of the Editor will be awarded the grand double prize, valued at one hundred pounds!

Each BEST that agrees with the Editor's gains five points, each NEXT BEST three points.

Enter now!

GROUP 1: Stories, Strips
A The Permit Weekend
B Pirate Island
C Salvation Army Story
D The Pony Patrol

GROUP 2: Articles
A Girls Would Be Boys
B So You've Won a Badge!
C Guiding on a Volcanic Island
D Guides in "Tom Thumb" Town
E Strange Incident
F Euroflags

GROUP 3: Things to Make
A Waterproof Cape and Hat
B For the Craft Badge
C Slipper Pincushion
D Maps That Mean Something

E Your Own Drinks

GROUP 4: Out of Doors
A All Kinds of Fires
B Facts About Fungi
C It's Grass Skiing
D Adventure With Rangers

GROUP 5: Puzzles, Quizzes
A Guess the Wildflower
B Flower and Plant Quiz
C The Kingfishers' Hike

GROUP 6: Local History Badge
A Story Behind the Field-Name
B Finding Firemarks
C False Fronts, Blocked Windows

THE GIRL GUIDE ANNUAL 1977 PRIZE COMPETITION ENTRY FORM

Simply write down the letter that is set against the title of your choice in the groups listed.

GROUP 1
Stories, BEST_____
Strips NEXT BEST_____

GROUP 2
Articles BEST_____
NEXT BEST_____

GROUP 3
Things to BEST_____
Make NEXT BEST_____

GROUP 4
Out of Doors
BEST_____
NEXT BEST_____

GROUP 5
Puzzles,
Quizzes BEST_____
NEXT BEST_____

GROUP 6
Local History Badge
BEST_____
NEXT BEST_____

Name and Address_____
_____
_____
_____

Age_____**Guide Company**
_____
_____

Guider's Name and Address_____
_____
_____
_____

91

The Girl Guide Annual 1977 Prize Competition

You can enter this exciting competition sure that you have an equal chance with every other competitor regardless of your age.

You may win the wonderful double prize of fifty pounds for your Company and something of your own choice to the value of £50 for yourself.

When you have made your choice of contributions and marked them on the entry form on the preceding page, think about what you like most in Guiding and write about it in a simple, straightforward way. You may like Guiding most for what you learn or for the friends it brings you or for the new activities it introduces to you. Whatever it is, tell about it in not more than about fifty words. Your write-up will be taken into account if there should be competitors with equal points who qualify for the prize.

When you have completed both front and back of the entry form, cut it out and post it to THE GIRL GUIDE ANNUAL 1977 PRIZE COMPETITION, PURNELL BOOKS, BERKSHIRE HOUSE, QUEEN STREET, MAIDENHEAD, BERKSHIRE, SL6 1NF.

Your entry must arrive not later than March 31st, 1977. The winner will be notified and the prize awarded as soon after this date as possible.

The publishers' decision is final, and no correspondence will be entered into in connection with the competition.

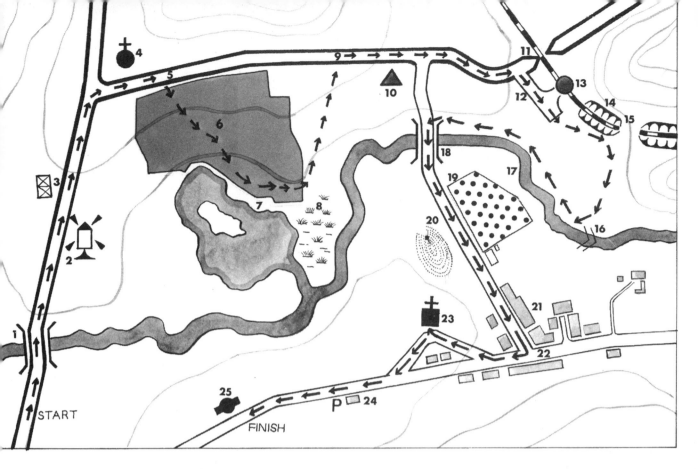

The Kingfishers' Hike

by Daphne Pilcher

By following the track can you tell by the Ordnance Survey symbols what the Kingfishers saw on their hike? Fill in the blanks in their report.

They got off the bus and walked over a __1__. On the right-hand side of the road they passed a __2__ and then on the left-hand side they had a look at some __3__. At a fork in the road they came across a __4__ with a __4__. Soon they left the __5__ road and went through a __6__ till they came to a __7__. They had to turn back because of __8__.

Back on the __9__ road they passed a __10__ __10__. They kept going till they reached a __11__ __11__. They turned down the __12__ __12__ that led to the __13__. Then they walked beside the __14__ till it went into a __15__. They had a look at the __16__, then they walked back along the __17__ bank till they came to a __18__ over it. On the way down the road they passed an __19__ on their left hand and a __20__ __20__ on their right. Before long they came to the __21__.

They went up the __22__ __22__ to the sixteenth-century __23__ with a __23__ and had a look round. They stopped at the __24__ __24__ to buy some postcards before they reached the __25__ __25__ where they caught the bus home.